DISTRACTIONS IN PRAYER:
BLESSING OR CURSE?

Visit our web site at
www.albahouse.org
(for orders www.alba-house.com)

or call 1-800-343-2522 (ALBA)
and request current catalog

Distractions in Prayer: Blessing or Curse?

St. Teresa of Avila's Teachings in *The Interior Castle*

VILMA SEELAUS, OCD

ST PAULS

Alba
House

Library of Congress Cataloging-in-Publication Data

Seelaus, Vilma.
  Distractions in prayer : blessing or curse? / Vilma Seelaus.
    p. cm.
  Includes bibliographical references.
  ISBN 0-8189-0985-4
1. Teresa, of Avila, Saint, 1515-1582. Moradas. 2. Spiritual life—Catholic
Church. 3. Prayer—Catholic Church.   I. Title.

  BX2179.T4S44 2005
  248.4'82—dc22
                                          2005005009

Produced and designed in the United States of America by the
Fathers and Brothers of the Society of St. Paul,
2187 Victory Boulevard, Staten Island, New York 10314-6603,
as part of their communications apostolate.

ISBN: 0-8189-0985-4

Printing Information:

Current Printing - first digit	1	2	3	4	5	6	7	8	9	10

Year of Current Printing - first year shown

2005	2006	2007	2008	2009	2010	2011	2012	2013	2014

TABLE OF CONTENTS

PREFACE

In 1985, the Carmelite Forum, of which I am a member, initiated
what has become an almost yearly Seminar on Carmelite Spirituality at St. Mary's College, Notre Dame, Indiana. Our intent is to
do as it were, a contemporary hermeneutic; to interpret for today's
understanding our Carmelite mystical tradition. At our very first
Seminar, each member of the Forum presented a workshop on
both St. Teresa of Avila and St. John of the Cross. Each of us also
conducted a reading session on a particular text and presented a
general lecture to the participants. At the end, we were exhausted.
That year we divided our forces. Some of us would specialize in
Teresa and some would do John of the Cross. It was hard to choose,
but I decided for Teresa. Each year, in preparation for the Seminar, I have read and reread a specific work of Teresa pursuing a
theme I intended to present at the Seminar the following year. As
a result, since 1985, Teresa has been my constant companion. As
a matter of fact, an almost life-size inspiring, original painting of
Teresa by the artist, Sister Marie Celeste of the Reno Carmel, hangs
in a prominent place near my office.[1] We are in frequent, silent

---

[1] The painting was intended for a Church dedicated to St. Teresa in Louisiana. The
priest who commissioned it started listening to my audio tapes on Teresa from
Alba House Publishers and, upon reflection, he decided that I was the one who
should have the painting. It has since been our privileged possession and it always
elicits deep feelings of gratitude toward the donor.

conversation with each other, often through a glance, as I pass by.
Over the years, I have presented workshops on each of
Teresa's major works. Much of this material is available through
Alba House Publishers who taped many of my lectures live. I enjoy pursuing a specific theme in Teresa's writings and then putting my theme in conversation, both with contemporary authors,
and with contemporary issues and understandings. Over the years,
as I reflected on the text, I noticed Teresa's frequent references to
distractions in prayer, especially in the various dwelling places in
her *Interior Castle*. This led to my preparing a workshop entitled,
"Distractions in Prayer, Blessings or Curse?" Teresa confirmed my
own experience that they are both! I also found that in each of
the dwelling places, Teresa had something unique to say about the
meaning of distractions and how best to deal with them. I also
found ways of interpreting the dwelling places that clarify them
for better contemporary understanding. I have presented this material a number of times in various settings and it has always received an enthusiastic response, which gave me confidence to further develop what I had begun.

I found that Lonergan's *fundamental forms of self-transcendence*, through levels of conversion seem to play themselves out,
especially in the early dwelling places as Teresa graphically depicts
the soul's struggle to begin the journey through the dwelling places.
Jacques Maritain's concept of the *spiritual unconscious* gave me a
language for explaining what Teresa does in *The Interior Castle*.
She maps the spiritual unconscious. The first dwelling places reflect the ways in which we tend to live outside of our true self.
What Teresa writes in the second dwelling places sounds like an
awakening to the more of life, while the third dwelling places easily
became rooms of complacency, by settling in for less. Here disillusionment can be grace. The fourth dwelling places are the rooms
of learning surrender, and so on.

The subtlety of distractions and their complexity of meanings surfaced as I delved deeper into the text. I discovered that distractions might actually be the voice of God inviting the person to deeper union with God, for as Rahner points out, "any intra-worldly reality or experience can be a moment of grace, a revelatory moment, because our experience of the divine within, of transcendental revelation, is always brought about or mediated through our being-in-the-world, through worldly experience."[2] God can indeed, and does communicate to us through our distractions.

My continued search disclosed the reality that distractions carry both information and energy for a deeper, truer love of God, of Christ and His gospel of love. Our interior journey takes us through many rooms in the interior castle, and some of the rooms are about God stretching the limits of human love for an ever-fuller divine manner of loving. In the process, we are faced with ongoing calls to ever-deeper levels of conversion and surrender to God's self-communication as our "worms" become "butterflies" and we become freer to be for others. But as we come closer to the inner rooms, we find that not only the mind, but also the *spirit*, borrowing from John of the Cross, can be distracted and in need of a purification which only God can effect through what John of the Cross calls the dark night of the spirit. In the sixth dwelling places, Teresa describes her own experience of the dark night. Here God uncovers for the soul's eye the root causes of distractions within the depth of the human *spirit*. Whatever is unloving, or substituting for God, finds exposure as God leads the soul into the silence of mystical speech. Here distractions can feel almost diabolic in nature as we face the depth of ourselves and learn to bear the bur-

---

[2] See Karl Rahner, "On the Theology of Worship," in *Theological Investigations*, vol. 19, Edward Quinn, trans. (New York: Crossroad, 1983), pp. 141-149. See also: "Grace and Religious Experience: The Everyday Mysticism of Karl Rahner," in *Master of the Sacred Page*, edited by Keith J. Egan, T.O.Carm. & Craig E. Morrison, O.Carm. (Washington, DC: Institute of Carmelite Studies, 1997), pp. 189-218.

den of our incompleteness and to allow Christ to make all things new. We come to discover that in Christ, all that is "of earth" in us is now also, "of God."

The seventh dwelling places find us finally at home in God and living habitually from our center. Here trials are not incompatible to a sense of abiding peace in God and holiness and imperfection are also at home with each other. Teresa calls the soul's experience of mutual self-giving with Christ, "becoming a slave of the crucified." Trials do not disturb its sense of abiding peace and the depth of its prayer releases the tranformative power of suffering. Having said no to what is less than God, and having been released from possessive self-grasp through surrender, the soul of Teresa is one with her God in spiritual marriage. The indwelling Trinity shines in habitual awareness in the soul of Teresa, and her life, now lived fully in Christ, becomes increasingly life-giving for others. This is our destiny also. Our distractions help situate us along the journey through the inner rooms of the castle to the room where "the king dwells" and where we too can increasingly become fruitful for others within today's context, and in response to today's needs.

I am grateful to Teresa for her guidance through the dwelling places. To insure that my inadequacies do not get in the way of fruitful reading, I pray intentionally each day, especially at our daily celebration of Eucharist, for anyone who may read what I have published over the years or who listen to my audio/video taped material. I am especially grateful to Father Kieran Kavanaugh, OCD, who after my initial workshop on Distractions, encouraged me to develop my material for a book. I have never felt motivated to get my ample material on Teresa into book form, but his words of encouragement sparked energy to pursue the project. I am also grateful for his comments and those of Kevin Culligan, OCD, in the early stages of my work. Commitment to my Carmelite life of prayer and involvement in community has slowed the process. A fall, which resulted in several pelvic fractures, kept me from my goal of finishing two summers ago. But here it is, and so I thank Mary M. Yascolt, OCD, my prioress, for her support and care, along with my community, with special thanks to Normagene Gillespie, OCD, our librarian, who checked my footnotes and citations. Friends encouraged me along the way. I am especially grateful to ST PAULS/Alba House for their enthusiastic response to my manuscript. With all of this, I can only say, (it will sound familiar to those who know me): *Praise God from whom all blessings flow!*

INTRODUCTION

In June 1577, in her monastery in Toledo, Spain, St. Teresa began writing *The Interior Castle* without any enthusiasm at all about the task given her. She felt no inspiration or desire to write about prayer. Her health was bad and she had many other business matters to attend to. In fact, she was undergoing one of the worst periods in her troubled history. The nuncio Ormaneto, who had favored Teresa's work, died during that very month, and the new nuncio, unfavorable to Teresa, was on his way to Spain. One idea, however, did give her strength to take up the endeavor. That was the thought that writing a new book on prayer was a chore given her by obedience. Beginning her work in June, while beset by a wave of disappointments in her life as a foundress, she continued until about the middle of July when she had to move to Avila. She had gotten as far as chapter two of the fifth dwelling place, probably writing chapter three in Avila in July. She then abandoned all work on her manuscript until the beginning of November. By November 29 her work was completed. Four days later her spiritual director, St. John of the Cross was taken prisoner, and on the following day she wrote her classic letter to the king pleading for help and justice on the saint's behalf. This is the time as well in which the nuns at the Incarnation who voted for her to be prioress again, notwithstanding warnings and threats, were excommunicated.

Despite these external clashes and her reluctance to begin this work, she actually enjoyed writing her book and ends, after working on it for only two and a half months, with an epilogue in which her mood sounds far better than in the prologue: "...now that I am finished I admit the work has brought me much happiness, and I consider the labor, though I confess it was small, well spent." In fact none of her troubles finds an echo in the work itself. It was written without any previous outlines or plans, as though she was in conversation with her sisters. The manuscript is preserved today in the Carmel of Seville as it came from her hands, as though it were but a prolonged and informal draft, without any divisions or chapter titles. But if written without previous outlines, the work was well thought out.

Once she got into writing the book, two motives for doing so urged her on. Twelve years previous to this, she had written *The Book of Her Life*. This manuscript was now in the possession of the Inquisition in Madrid. Though the examiners found no reason for condemnation, they did not think it wise for a book of such a nature to be passed around, and so kept it out of circulation. But Teresa thought that she had managed to explain some matters about prayer for her nuns very well and was afraid her pages would be lost forever. The second motive was that her spiritual life had developed further since she had written previously. A whole new stage, her final one, the most peaceful one in her mystical life, needed to be expounded. Father Gracián, her superior at the time, thought it would be best for her to write another book dealing with many of the same matters she treated in her *Life* and also the new material. But this time she was not to present her thought in an autobiographical manner as in the *Life*. She tried then to present her material more objectively, often presenting personal matters as though happening to somebody she knew.

On the first page of her manuscript these words appear: "Teresa of Jesus, a nun of Our Lady of Mount Carmel, wrote this treatise called *The Interior Castle* for her sisters and daughters, the discalced Carmelite nuns." As time went on this book was published and translated into many languages. It is a classic that has kept the name given on the first page of the manuscript: *The Interior Castle*. The castle is above all Teresa's castle, her soul, her life. It is as well the Lord's castle. But it serves also as a kind of lookout point from which the reader may see into his own castle, because Teresa, from the outset, is interested in setting up a kind of drawbridge between the two castles, hers and ours. Out of her own experience she enters our castle guiding and urging us forward, always with deep love and respect. In fact the entire work is a testimony to the dignity of each human being, a dwelling place for God, an interior castle with many rooms: "some up above, others down below, others to the sides; and in the center and middle is the main dwelling place where the secret exchanges between God and the soul take place."

As is well known the door of entry to the castle is prayer. And Teresa as she leads us through the castle presents an entire treatise on the spiritual life from the viewpoint of prayer and its development. A great deal of commentary has been written on this archetypal work of Teresa's, but no one has approached the work as Sister Vilma does. If we have read *The Interior Castle* before, we will read it now as though it is an entirely new book. Sister Vilma takes us through the castle from the viewpoint of our distractions. Distractions are, after all, the major problem in anyone's prayer, and this is why it is so important to have a commentator of the author's depth guide us through Teresa's castle from this one perspective: distractions, their meaning for us in our spiritual lives. It is Sister Vilma's conviction that Teresa's insights to the dwelling places of the soul alert us to the meaning of our distractions. As we reflect with her, we begin to see how instead of being a curse, our distractions are a blessing, a visitation from God. Journeying again through the castle and looking at distractions and their meaning through this prism of the seven dwelling places, we will listen with fresh insight to the voices of these distractions and will then even learn to welcome them as integral to God's transforming process.

Kieran Kavanaugh, OCD

ABBREVIATIONS

The Collected Works of St. Teresa of Avila, trans. Kieran Kavanaugh and Otilio Rodriguez, Washington, DC: Institute of Carmelite Studies. This publisher is cited as ICS. Abbreviations are supplied for frequently cited works of Teresa of Avila, John of the Cross and Thérèse of Lisieux.

Note the study edition of *The Way of Perfection*. ICS, 2000.

Vol. 1 (1976):	*The Book of Her Life*	BL
Vol. 2 (1980):	*The Way of Perfection*	WP
	The Interior Castle	IC
Vol. 3 (1985):	*The Book of Her Foundations*	BF

The Collected Works of St. John of the Cross, revised edition, trans. Kieran Kavanaugh and Otilio Rodriguez, Washington, DC: ICS, 1991. Below are abbreviations for commentaries. Letters are cited as Letter with number of the letter.

The Ascent of Mount Carmel	A
The Dark Night	DN
The Spiritual Canticle	SC
The Living Flame of Love	LF
The Sayings of Light and Love	SL

Story of a Soul: The Autobiography of St. Thérèse of Lisieux, 3rd ed., trans. John Clarke. Washington, DC: ICS, 1996.

Story of a Soul	SS

DISTRACTIONS IN PRAYER:
BLESSING OR CURSE?

SETTING THE STAGE
The Mystery of Human-God-Relatedness

The Spiritual Canticle by John of the Cross, which is a dramatic poem of a lover in search of her beloved, begins with the lover's anguished cry: "Where have you hidden, Beloved, and left me moaning?" Deep within each of us is a relentless desire for God the Beloved, who alone satisfies the soul's deepest longings. And yet, our experience in prayer would have us paraphrase John's words with our own anguished cry: Where have you hidden, Beloved, *and left me to my distractions?* In the gospel story of the prodigal son, the father reminds his complaining firstborn: "Son, you I have always with me." Distractions, like the elder son, truly are always with us. They dutifully perform an important service that calls for recognition and for reassurance that God welcomes them with the same caring, transforming welcome extended to the prodigal son. Teresa of Avila will help us to see the importance of our distractions for spiritual transformation. Through the prism of her *Interior Castle*, we discover that within the many faceted dwelling places of the soul distractions offer opportunities for increased self-knowledge, along with occasions for deepened commitment to the One who welcomes us, distractions and all. Since distractions are indeed always with us, the goal of prayer is not to rid ourselves of them. To attempt to completely rid oneself of distractions in prayer could prove to be another form of distraction. God can and does awe the soul into inner stillness, and there are techniques that help us to realize quiet mindfulness, but all too frequently we continue to struggle with distractions in prayer.

As a common component of prayer, distractions call our attention to the stream of consciousness that is integral to the workings of the psyche.[1] This stream of consciousness is part of the human reality and it means that we are alive. As a characteristic of being human, distractions are creatures of God. God speaks to us through them even as God speaks to us through all of God's creation. Distractions can serve therefore, as a "word of God" inviting us to greater self-knowledge and to deeper surrender of the mind and heart to God. God uses every opportunity to bring us to loving knowledge both of God and of oneself. Distractions offer genuine openings to a fuller life in God. They often mirror deep realities held within the human heart. They can reflect our values and the things we hold precious. They can also reveal with glaring truth our attachments, and our personal, unique vulnerability to sin. At the same time, the distress we feel because of our distractions, expresses the heart's desire for God that co-exists with our inner conflicts.

The seven dwelling places of Teresa's *Interior Castle* focus on the heart's desire for union with God. Teresa here attends to God's part in our prayer because, in her experience, "only what we ourselves can do in prayer is explained to us: little is explained about what the Lord does in a soul" (I.7).[2] However, in explain-

---

[1] See "Contemplation and Stream of Consciousness" by Kieran Kavanaugh in *Carmel and Prayer: A Tradition for the 21st Century* (New York/Mahwah, NJ: Paulist Press, 2003), p. 101 ff.

[2] All references to the works of Teresa of Avila or John of the Cross are taken from the translation by Kieran Kavanaugh and Otilio Rodriguez, OCD (Washington, DC: Institute of Carmelite Studies).

ing what the Lord does, Teresa, at the same time, helps us to understand what is our part in our prayer-relationship with God. This becomes particularly true in the matter of distractions. Woven into her text are both hints and pointers to different kinds of distractions characteristic of each dwelling place. Not only does she give advice on how to deal with them, she also interprets their meaning for our spiritual growth.

As we walk through these seven dwelling places, with their myriad of rooms, we see our lives and our distractions uniquely reflected in each room. What follows is an attempt to ferret out the various levels of distractions, and their different meanings, as we find them within the dwelling places of Teresa's *Interior Castle*. Through interpretative understanding of these dwelling places, and Teresa's insightful remarks about distractions, we can listen with fresh insight to the voices of our own distractions and discover their transforming potential.

Teresa's words about that which distracts us from reaching the center room claim our attention as we journey inward through the many rooms of the castle. Because we are so easily distracted from our purpose, within Teresa's exposition of the dwelling places is God's invitation to ever-deeper levels of conversion. Teresa insists that "there is a great difference in the ways one may be inside the castle" (I.1.5). Each of the dwelling places contains a call to greater integrity, and therefore to conversion of heart, to a more complete turning of one's entire self toward God. God, who is always present to the soul as abiding offer of love, awakens the soul's need for ongoing moral, intellectual, and religious conversion, which is to say, to an ever deeper falling in love with God.[3] In this ongoing process of conversion, Teresa helps us to understand both the ubiquity of distractions and the

---

[3] Bernard Lonergan, *Method in Theology* (New York: Seabury Press, 1972; San Francisco: HarperSF, 1985). See especially, p. 237 ff.

gift that they can be toward needed growth in self-knowledge, conversion of heart, and loving surrender to God.

A rather lengthy, but key text found in chapter one of the fourth dwelling place sets the stage for reflecting on the dwelling places. In this dwelling place Teresa concerns herself with the transition from meditation to contemplation. She writes:

> O Lord, take into account the many things we suffer on this path for lack of knowledge! The trouble is that since we do not think there is anything to know other than that we must think of You, we do not even know how to ask those who know nor do we understand what there is to ask. Terrible trials are suffered because we don't understand ourselves, and that which isn't bad at all but good we think is a serious fault. This lack of knowledge causes the afflictions of many people who engage in prayer; complaints about interior trials, at least to a great extent, by people who have no learning; melancholy and loss of health; and even the complete abandonment of prayer. For such persons don't reflect that there is an interior world here within us. **Just as we cannot stop the movement of the heavens, but they proceed in rapid motion, so neither can we stop our mind; and then the faculties of the soul go with it, and we think that we are lost and have wasted the time spent before God** [Emphasis mine]. But the soul is perhaps completely joined with him in the dwelling places very close to the center while the mind is on the outskirts of the castle suffering from a thousand wild and poisonous beasts, and meriting by this suffering. As a result we should not be disturbed nor should we abandon prayer, which

is what the devil wants us to do. For the most part all the trials and disturbances come from our not understanding ourselves (IV.1.9).

Teresa's focus on the need for self-understanding, for self-knowledge in relation to trials and disturbances, bears reflection: "We suffer because of our lack of knowledge." John of the Cross has similar things to say, namely, that the practice of self-knowledge is the first requirement of advancing to the knowledge of God (SC 4.1). He also says that "trials preserve the soul in humility and self-knowledge" (DN 1.14.5). The nights of the soul expose us to ourselves as God makes room for God within the human heart. In *The Living Flame*, the flame of God's love initially causes suffering; it is not bright but dark.

Neither is the flame refreshing and peaceful, but it is consuming and contentious, making a person faint and suffer with self-knowledge. Thus it is not glorious for the soul, but rather makes it feel wretched and distressed in the spiritual light of self-knowledge that it bestows. As Jeremiah declares, "God sends fire into its bones and instructs it" [Lm 1:13]; and as David also asserts, "He tries it with fire" [Ps 17:3] (LF1.19).

As we shall see, distractions are an invaluable source of self-knowledge, but in the process, they try us with fire! God will work through them for our soul's transformation if we can be open to the inner work they call forth from us.

Self-Knowledge: What We Need to Know about Ourselves
The Presence of God to Human Life

Essential to self-knowledge is awareness of God's intimate presence to human life.

Primitive cave drawings, the sacred books of world religions, the writings of the mystics, the present-day revival of spirituality are all of a piece in the unfolding of God in human life. In his masterful three-volume *History of Religious Ideas* Mircea Eliade shows that *the sacred* is an element in the very structure of human consciousness; it is not something that evolved in time. The most archaic and ancient level of culture considered everything a religious act. Food-getting, sexual life and work all had a sacramental value. Eliade concludes that to be human signifies being "religious."[4]

The dynamic of prayer as an innate desire for God is rooted in the human psyche. God is not *out there* in far-off heavens. The mystery of God unfolds from *within* and is supported by all the external events of life. Such is Teresa's self-understanding: her person, God, prayer, and life are all interwoven. John of the Cross supports Teresa in this understanding. In speaking about the substantial union of the soul with God, he writes:

> To understand the nature of this union, one should
> first know that God sustains every soul and dwells in

---

[4]   Eliade, the great philosopher and historian of world religions, claims that within the human, "consciousness of a real and meaningful world is intimately connected with the discovery of the sacred. Through experience of the sacred, the human mind has perceived the difference between what reveals itself as being real, powerful, rich and meaningful and what lacks these qualities, that is, the chaotic and dangerous flux of things, their fortuitous and senseless appearances and differences. In short, the 'sacred' is an element in the structure of consciousness and not a stage in the history of consciousness." Out of this innate sense of the sacred, world religions develop and spiritual traditions come into existence. Mircea Eliade, *A History of Religious Ideas*, trans. by Willard R. Trask (Chicago: University of Chicago Press, 1982, Vol. 1).

it substantially, even though it may be that of the greatest sinner in the world. This union between God and the creature always exists (A2.5).[5]

Without this substantial union with God, we would cease to be. Both our existence and our identity are relational; we receive both from God. Our entire being is a mystery of human-God relatedness. In stanza 11.3 of the *Spiritual Canticle* John of the Cross explains that God's presence is of three kinds. First: God's presence by essence, or God's substantial presence in every person by which God gives us life and being. Second: God's presence by grace in which, as John puts it, God abides in the soul pleased and satisfied. Third: God's presence by what John calls *spiritual affection*. He writes: "God grants his spiritual presence to devout souls in many ways by which he refreshes, delights and gladdens them." John refers here to a profound level of interactive presence. Identifying these modes of God's presence, from the essential presence to mystical union, helps to determine how we deal with subsequent levels of distraction that assail us in prayer.

Karl Rahner demonstrates a profound grasp of our human transcendental orientation. He maintains that we always experience more of ourselves at the non-thematic and non-reflexive levels in the ultimate and fundamental living of our life than we know about ourselves by reflecting upon ourselves. We can intuit things about ourselves deeper than the mind can grasp. Writing about the experience of self and the experience of God as one reality, Rahner makes the daring assertion:

---

[5] John of the Cross points out that there is another union, transformation in likeness of love where the soul will be clothed in a new understanding of God in God and in a new love of God. (A1.5.7)

> The transcendental orientation of man [the human person] to the incomprehensible and ineffable Mystery which constitutes the enabling condition for knowledge and freedom, and therefore for subjective life as such, in itself implies a real, albeit a non-thematic experience of God.

A person may know nothing of theology or of the self-revelatory word of God, nevertheless, writes Rahner:

> ...while the experience of God and experience of self are not simply identical, still both of them exist with a unity of such a kind that apart from this unity it is quite impossible for there to be any such experiences at all.

He continues:

> This unity consists far more in the fact that the original and ultimate experience of God constitutes the enabling condition of, and an intrinsic element in, the experience of self in such a way that without this experience of God no experience of self is possible. In other words the personal history of the experience of God signifies, over and above itself, the personal history of the experience of the self.[6]

Important to the spiritual journey is that we grasp the profound reality of Rahner's thought. God's substantial or essential

---

6 Karl Rahner, "Experience of Self and Experience of God" in *Theological Investigations*, vol. 13, David Burke, trans. (New York: Crossroad, 1983), p. 122 ff.

presence to human life is a presence so intimate that without it we cease to exist. Our transcendent functions of consciousness and freedom flow from the ultimate transcendence that is ours in the essential union of our soul with God. As Rahner rightly asserts, although our experience of God and experience of the self each constitute themes in their own right, without the experience of God no experience of self is possible. Sebastian Moore describes self-awareness as "the trace or vestige of God."[7] Jacques and Raissa Maritain, who lived in the middle of the last century, furthered human self-understanding useful in dealing with distractions. Under the impetus of the discovery of the psychological unconscious, and their own research into the nature of faith and mystical experience, the Maritains began to see that the various kinds of knowledge by connaturality, like intuition and the creative process, as well as contemplation, are all rooted in what they called the spiritual unconscious. This is the natural spiritual depth of the soul, which grace transforms into what could be called a supernatural unconscious. From the depth of his supernatural unconscious erupts this lyric outpouring of John of the Cross:

> Oh, then, soul, most beautiful among all creatures, so anxious to know the dwelling place of your Beloved so you may go in search of him and be united with him, now we are telling you that you yourself are his dwelling and his secret inner room and hiding place. There is reason for you to be elated and joyful in seeing that all your good and hope is so close as to be within you or better, that you cannot be without him.

---

[7] Sebastian Moore, *The Fire and the Rose Are One* (New York: Seabury Press, 1980), p. 120.

"Behold," exclaims the Bridegroom, *"the kingdom of God is within you"* [Lk 17:21]. And his servant, the apostle St. Paul declares: *"You are the temple of God"* [2 Cor 6:16] (SC1.7).[8]

Mapping the Supernatural Unconscious
Teresa's *Interior Castle*

What Maritain calls the supernatural unconscious, Teresa charts for us room by room in the journey through the dwelling places. Skillfully, she guides us into the inner world of the spirit. She cheers us on as we search the text of her classic among mystical writings, the *Interior Castle*. With the eyes of the heart, we look for contemporary understandings that give meaning for our lives today. Distractions that are unique to each dwelling place, and their appropriate response, help focus our approach to the text. In doing so, with Teresa, we turn to the one whom she calls *the good Jesus* in whom God's essential presence within the human finds visibility. We look to him to companion us as we journey through the dwelling places, because in Jesus, God is embodied. Our flesh and our spirit, even our distractions, are in continuity with his. It is Jesus who speaks most convincingly of divine indwelling and of our inherence in him as the vine inheres the branches. God's Trinitarian life finds a home in us in a mutual abiding.

---

8   For a fine summary of the mystery that is the human person see stanza one of the *Spiritual Canticle*. John of the Cross helps us to understand why we suffer at times in our prayer-relationship with God. This chapter provides a good introduction to Teresa's *Interior Castle*.

A Journey Through the Castle

We begin with the obvious: Teresa's Interior Castle is no ordinary castle. It is like a crystal diamond, says Teresa, or like a palmetto plant that has many leaves surrounding and covering the center that alone is edible. The center is God.[9] Each of the many passages that describe the dwelling places adds further nuance to the castle-soul through the effects of sinful living to the soul finding itself *in God* whose vital, global presence *"castles"* the soul.[10] The dwelling places show the dynamic of our prayer-relationship with God as a concentric movement toward the center room. As Rahner puts it:

> The center of all reality, the innermost heart of all infinity, the love of the all-holy God has become our center, our heart. True and absolute reality now lives in our nothingness; the strength of God vitalizes our weakness; eternal life lives in mortal human beings.[11]

The pull is inward toward the center room, but once secure in the embrace of the all-holy, self-giving Trinitarian God the soul necessarily expands and reaches outward toward others, as is the nature of God.[12]

I am reminded of the ocean tides that wash the beach near our monastery here in Rhode Island. The waters overflow the sands, and at a very high tide, even the marshlands are flooded.

---

[9] Key passages that describe the Castle are: I.1.1; I.1.3; I.1.5; I.2.8; and VI.10.3.

[10] See VI.7.2-3, where Teresa sees all things *in God.*

[11] Karl Rahner, *The Great Church Year* edited by Albert Raffelt (New York: Crossroad, 1993), p. 211. The notion of *the center* is a very archetypal image. See Mircea Eliade: *The History of World Religions*, Vol. 2, pp. 42-43; also p. 402.

[12] See Hans Urs Von Balthasar in *The Trinity and the Paschal Mystery* by Ann Hunt, New Theology Series, 5 (Collegeville, MN: The Liturgical Press, 1997).

But soon the waters inch back for periods of shore-line containment that characterizes low tide until the tides again surge forward. Like the movement of the tides that come and go, the journey to the center room is not linear. We are never so fully within a dwelling place that the waters of the soul do not recede to rooms already visited. A kind of fluidity characterizes the soul. We easily move in and out of the different rooms even though the soul might basically be settled in a particular place at a given time. Teresa wisely observes:

> You must not think, sisters, that the effects I mentioned are always present in these souls. [Teresa refers to things like forgetfulness of self and spiritual joys that are characteristic of the seventh dwelling place (VII.2.2-10).] For, sometimes our Lord leaves these individuals in their natural state, and then it seems all the poisonous creatures from the outskirts and other dwelling places of this castle band together to take revenge for the time they were unable to have these souls under their control (VII.4.1).

Teresa insists that the castle of the soul is vast. She focuses on only seven significant rooms in our journey toward the center room, although as Teresa writes in her *Epilogue*, #3, "The rooms are so many that you would want to be dissolved in praises of the great God who created the soul in His own image and likeness." The journey toward intimacy with God draws us beyond our conceived limits and stretches us to the fullest and highest realms of the human potential. With profound insight, Teresa finds the center of the world within herself. Or more accurately, God reveals to Teresa the depth of her own mystery. Within the soul is an ever-expanding universe like a magnificent, yet mysterious castle with countless rooms.

Today the insights of physicists expand Teresa's understanding of the connection between the inner and the outer world. The physicist, Brian Swimme, with a vision akin to the mystics, projects the universe as becoming conscious of itself through the evolution of human life. As Swimme puts it: "The universe shivers with wonder in the depths of the human." Billions of years prepare planet earth for life and for the development of human consciousness. Swimme understands the process of evolution as the universe in search of itself; our appearance as humans allows the universe to move to a deeper level, as matter, the material world, begins to see itself through human eyes.[13] I would add that the universe, centered in the human, now searches for its heart, the living God, who is the flame of love that energizes, transforms, and glorifies all existence. The universe in search of itself is now one reality with the human search for God.

Like a blinding sun breaking through clouds, Teresa's castle image breaks through our myopic view of the human to tease us toward a vision of ourselves in which we see both our human/divine complexity and our human/divine potential. Distractions in prayer and in life, are part of the integration process as the reality of human, cosmic, divine inter-connectedness works itself toward fullness and harmony within fragile, human finitude. We do not easily carry the burden of divine Presence nor do we easily accept personal responsibility for planet earth, which is our share in the evolving universe. I suggest that within Teresa's descriptions of the dwelling places can be found insight for relating to distractions particular not only to Teresa's life and times but also to the many pulls of our fragmented, alienated postmodern world.

---

[13] Brian Swimme, *The Universe Is a Green Dragon: A Cosmic Creation Story* (Santa Fe, NM: Bear & Co., 1984), p. 32 ff.

CHAPTER ONE

THE FIRST DWELLING PLACES

The outer rooms of the castle and the first dwelling places are about the human proclivity toward superficial living. God is not taken seriously in these first dwelling places, even though the person occasionally prays. The center room of the divine self is boarded up with superficialities; such a person lives outside of the true self. This dwelling place epitomizes over-involvement in worldly affairs and pleasure seeking — regardless of the cost to others — as one's ultimate goal in life. Here things like: ambition, ruthless getting ahead, money, success, sex, provide the drive of life. God's invitation to full humanity in Christ is misdirected into temporal realities, into things good in themselves, but which diminish us if these become our total preoccupation. Teresa describes with vivid imagery the anatomy of such deformations:

> Persons who do not practice prayer are like people with paralyzed or crippled bodies; even though they have hands and feet they cannot give orders to these hands and feet (I.1.6).

For Teresa, mortal sin is the epitome of human deformation. In the seventh dwelling places, speaking of mortal sin, she pictures a man with his hands tied behind his back with a strong chain, bound to a post and dying of hunger, not because of lack of food, for there are choice dishes beside him, but because he cannot take hold of the food and eat, and even has a great loathing for it (VII.1.4).[1] According to Teresa, to be totally outside of one's center is a living hell. Coldness and indifference toward others characterize such a life. Anything that leads "to a cooling of charity and love" (I.2.17) leaves us precariously near the outskirts of the castle, "in serious danger" (I.1.7). I think here of one of the scenes in Dante's *Inferno*. Virgil leads Dante to Hell's deepest sphere, the frozen lake of Cocytus that is peopled with those who allow a cold, cruel egotism gradually to strike inward till even the lingering passions of hatred are frozen into immobility. They have so damned themselves by their denial of heartwarming human values that they are up to their necks and held in paralyzing cold.[2] Theirs is the ultimate in a self-absorption that leads to unrelieved, unredeemable isolation as C.S. Lewis so graphically describes in *The Great Divorce*. For Lewis, hell is always having your own way.[3] We resist being disturbed in our willfulness even by God.

Distractions in the First Dwelling Places

Willfulness and the cooling of charity pave a slippery path to a hell that we fashion for ourselves because there is no exchange of life with God or with others that results in transfor-

---

[1] See I.2.1-4 for another description of the soul in mortal sin.

[2] Helen M. Luke, *Dark Wood, White Rose* (Pecos, NM: Dove Publications, 1975), p. 35.

[3] C.S. Lewis, *The Great Divorce* (New York: Macmillan Co., 1946; New York: Simon & Schuster Touchstone Trade Paperback, 1996; Nashville, TN: Broadman, 1999).

mation. In these first dwelling places distractions are an ever-present reality enticing the person toward the desired object. At the same time, distractions are not a conscious issue because such persons rarely pray, and when they do, often the mind is not in the heart. Persons pray "without considering or understanding whom you are speaking with, or as you approach, with whom you are about to speak."[4] Prayer is mere formality because the heart is too absorbed in temporal realities. "A prayer in which a person is not aware of whom he is speaking to, what he is asking, who it is who is asking and of whom, I do not call prayer, however much the lips move" (I.1.7). To be thus absorbed in temporal realities is to live outside of the true self because one is outside of the awareness of human-God-relatedness. Anything that keeps us stuck in superficial living is a first dwelling place experience. Fortunately, like distractions, God too is always present, nudging us beyond the cooling of charity, toward the warmth of God. Teresa says that this room is bright but a person doesn't enjoy it because of the impediment of things like "these wild animals or beasts," which symbolize absorption in worldly affairs (I.2.14).

No matter the intensity of our spiritual path, no one is exempt from temptations in first dwelling place experiences, prompted, as Teresa would have it, by the devil. Persons in this dwelling place may not be in a bad state. They are simply "over-involved and absorbed in temporal matters" (I.2.14). Being attuned to the voice of our distractions alerts us to God's invitation to inner freedom.

Although her nuns are free from the snares of material gain, they too can experience the same kind of distracting tumult, but

---

[4] *Way of Perfection*, 22.7. Teresa insists throughout this work on the importance of mindfulness of God both in prayer and in life.

for different reasons. They may be free with respect to exterior matters; "In interior matters may it please the Lord that we also be free, and may He free us" (I.2.15). There are few dwelling places in this castle in which the devil does not wage battle; "He may deceive us by changing himself into an angel of light," warns Teresa. No matter how intent we may be in our desire for God, or detached from *external* things, temptations in *interior* matters are always a possibility. First dwelling place distractions may be an indiscreet zeal that leaves one distracted and critical about other people who do not measure up to our standards of behavior, or whose values may differ from ours, if such thoughts lead to a cooling of charity toward one's neighbor. We may experience the same kind of distractions in other dwelling places, but they do not lead to a cooling of charity for, as Teresa wisely observes, "the guards (which I believe I have said, are the faculties) have the strength to fight" (I.2.15). Teresa notes that hardly any light coming from the king's royal chamber reaches these first dwelling places. The soul is very close to the snakes, vipers, and poisonous creatures, symbols of our attachments and lack of inner freedom, so our distracting temptations have the potential for serious soul-harm. Anything that leads to a cooling of charity in oneself or others is a serious matter. Teresa wants us to realize that the devil uses many wiles and deceits so that souls may not know themselves or understand their own paths (I.2.12). Her nuns are good women whom "the devil deceives by changing himself into an angel of light." The devil distracts one nun with impulses toward penance done without permission so that she ruins her health. He imbues another with such zeal that she follows every little fault the sisters commit and makes them a serious breach. She carefully observes whether they commit them, and then informs the prioress. In the process, she doesn't see her own faults. A habit of projecting on to others our own unacknowledged darkness ranging from sin to human limitation keeps the psyche grounded in the first dwelling places. To be obsessed with critical thoughts of others invites a deeper look into our own patterns of denial and lack of self-awareness.[5]

Teresa's reference to excessive penances has implications for us today. Excessive penance that ruins health is hardly our problem; ours is the other extreme of over-indulgence that also ruins health. We internalize the allurements of the advertising world and these become compulsive needs. A self-centered will-fulness demands that we do "our thing" regardless of the advice of others. In these dwelling places thoughts that lead to the *cooling of charity*, in their extreme, slide into character assassination of others, lack of forgiveness, and potential violence. They also lead to serious addictive patterns, harmful to us. This is the potential room of closet narcissism where walls of alienation are built of self-pity and perpetual victimhood.

Teresa's concluding advice in her discussion of the first dwelling places focuses on keeping a perspective that fosters love of self and of others and that lets trifles be trifles. First dwelling place distractions are invasive distractions that keep us stuck in superficialities and blind us to our own faults, that cause us to lose our peace and to disturb the peace of others, to plan retaliation, to be unforgiving of ourselves and others, in short, all thoughts that lead *to a cooling of charity* (I.2.18).

---

[5] In *Will and Spirit: A Contemplative Psychology* (San Francisco, CA: Harper & Row, 1982), Gerald May has an insightful chapter entitled "Encounter with Evil," pp. 265-296. This chapter explicates things akin to those in Teresa's first dwelling places.

CHAPTER TWO

THE SECOND DWELLING PLACES

The second dwelling places are the rooms of awakening to the "more" of life. An inner stirring awakens faith and moves the will towards God. "Such persons," writes Teresa, "begin to practice prayer but they do not avoid occasions of sin," which, as Teresa wisely comments, "is very dangerous." To the extent that the soul responds to God, worldly desires and desire for God come into conflict. Such persons tend to rise and fall (II.1.2,9).

> This stage pertains to those who have already begun to practice prayer and have understood how important it is not to stay in the first dwelling places. But they still don't have the determination to remain in this second stage without turning back, for they don't avoid the occasions of sin.

But God, ever faithful, pursues the wavering heart:

> Since they are getting closer to where His Majesty dwells, He is a very good neighbor. His mercy and goodness are so bountiful; whereas we are occupied in our pastimes, business affairs, pleasures, and worldly buying and selling, and still falling into sin and rising again (II.1.2).

Conflicting desires cause the person to rise and fall even as the tides of divine love inch their way into previously uncontested regions of the psyche where worldly desires held sway. These archetypical *beasts*, as Teresa calls worldly matters, "are so dangerous and **noisy** (emphasis mine) that it would be a wonder if we kept from stumbling and falling over them" (II.1.2).

Persons in this dwelling space are at a critical threshold in their life with God, although Teresa's exposition is brief because, as she reminds us, she "has spoken at length on this subject elsewhere." She refers to chapters eleven and twelve of *The Book of Her Life*. What she says in *The Life* about the first degree of prayer sheds light on the struggles of the second dwelling places. Consistent to both, is the importance of Christ in the spiritual journey. Teresa would have us "be where His Majesty dwells." She insists that, "He is a very good neighbor and his mercy and goodness is bountiful. He desires intensely that we love Him and seek His company, so much so, that from time to time He call us to draw near Him" (II.2). Christ's presence creates energy toward moral conversion as new horizons of intimacy with Christ open up. Dim to the soul's eye as Christ may be in this second dwelling place, since the person does not avoid occasions of sin, still the heart is moved toward moral conversion. According to Lonergan, moral conversion implies that the criterion of one's decisions and choices slowly shifts from narcissistic self-satisfaction and immersion in worldly pleasure to human values that take into account the good of others.

> One frees oneself from the inauthentic. One grows in authenticity. Harmful, dangerous misleading satisfactions are dropped. Fears of discomfort, pain and privation have less power to deflect one from one's

course. Values are apprehended where before they were overlooked. Scales of preference shift.[1]

Here, distractions in prayer come as images of the desired good since addictions/attachments still have a strong hold on the psyche. In *The Life*, Teresa comes to the heart of things: our illusion is "that we are giving all to God, whereas the truth of the matter is that we are paying God the rent or giving Him the fruits and keeping for ourselves the ownership and the root" (*Life*, II.2). The struggle is around manipulative possession of the world around us, which is intended for our use, but not to be clung to as an absolute value. For Teresa, the litmus test of inner freedom in this dwelling place is the degree of *anxiety* we experience around fear of losing either possessions or status. *Excessive* anxiety, like all strong feelings, distracts the heart from becoming a servant of love, which is the goal Teresa sets before us (*Life*, II.1-2).

John of the Cross describes the soul's struggle toward inner freedom. He also artfully describes the benefits of the struggle. "By withdrawing joy from sensible things, individuals are restored from the **distraction** into which they had fallen through excessive uses of their senses. They become recollected in God and conserve the spirit and virtues they had acquired" (A3.26.2). Here John explains that many of our attachments/addictions are connected with sense pleasure. They create inner pressure as desire for whatever we are addicted to and they cause persistent **distractions** (emphasis mine).

In A3.22.2, John offers a graphic description of the harm that comes from what he calls "joy of will in natural goods." He elaborates six principles of harm. The *first* includes things such

---

[1] Bernard Lonergan, SJ, *Method in Theology* (New York: Seabury Press, 1972), pp. 52, 240.

as vainglory, presumption, pride and disesteem of neighbor; the
second harm centers around whatever incites the senses to complacency, sensual delight and lust; the *third* kind of harm is that
which induces flattery and vain praises; the *fourth* kind is general, for the reason and judgment of the spirit become very dull;
the *fifth* gives rise to **distractions** of the mind with creatures; the
sixth causes the soul to find extreme tedium and sadness in the
things of God, even to the extent of abhorring them. Conse-
quently, the soul lives more in the weakness of the senses than
in the strength it has when occasions of sin arise. Even if the spirit
is unaware of any harm, **distraction** is at least secretly caused.

Desire is always a relational energy. It directs itself toward
a person or thing perceived to be a good not possessed, or not
sufficiently in possession. In the passage above, John writes of
the dark side of desire that entices us to give persons and things
an absolute value. We look to them to fill an emptiness that in
fact is space for God. When we give created realities the impossible task of usurping divine prerogatives, they rebel by leading
us into the distortions of the human called sin, the effects of
which John describes above. For Teresa, the remedy against
temptation is prayer; the "door of entry into this castle is prayer"
(II.11). Through prayer, human weakness becomes a sure access
to God. All that is human, including human weakness, is mysteriously in God through the wounded, dying and risen Christ.
Where sin abounds, Christ is all the more present. We will return to this theme in the later dwelling places.

In Christ, God remains intimate to our deepest need. In
prayer, the life-giving Spirit of Jesus illumines the dark corners
of the heart. The images, thoughts, and feelings that are part of
the ever-present stream of consciousness that intrudes on our
prayer, illumined by the Spirit of Jesus, divulge content for conversion of heart. When the distracting thoughts of the mind and
the misdirected desires of the heart become vulnerable before

God, they act as transparencies to God's transforming love and invite conversion of heart. Recurring thoughts and feelings here serve as the word of God, urging conversion to inner freedom for a deeper falling in love with God. Teresa concludes her discussion of the second dwelling places with a simple method of recollection:

> Well now, it is foolish to think that we will enter heaven without entering into ourselves, coming to know ourselves, reflecting on our misery and what we owe God, and begging Him often for mercy (II.1.11).[2]

Christ remains central to Teresa's method of prayer:

> Well, if we never look at Him or reflect on what we owe Him and the death He suffered for us, I don't know how we'll be able to know Him or do works in His service. And what value can faith have without works and without joining them to the merits of Jesus Christ, our Good? Or who will awaken us to love this Lord? (II.1.11).

Bernard Lonergan suggests that in moral conversion, when a person learns to opt for the truly good, even for value in preference to satisfaction when value and satisfaction conflict, at this stage one has to remain ready to learn from others.[3] Teresa concurs. To turn away from bad companions, she advises that we "draw near not only to those seen to be in these rooms where he is but to those known to have entered the ones closer to the center. Conversation with these latter will be a great help to him

---

[2] See: *The Book of Her Life*, ch. II. Here Teresa describes the first degree of prayer under the image of the four ways of watering the garden of the soul.

[3] Bernard Lonergan, *op. cit.*, p. 140.

and he can converse so much with them that they will bring him to where they are" (II.1.6). Good spiritual guidance is vital to this dwelling place. Psychotherapy, twelve step programs, and other therapeutic adjuncts can also lead toward insight and freedom from the diminishing effects of disordered desire that have roots deep in the psyche, and which cause disturbances in the mind, and havoc in the emotions. Humility, prayer, and a willingness to live with the pain of facing our un-freedoms, are important at this time. For as Teresa wisely remarks, "We have no better weapon than that of the cross" (II.1.6).

In these second dwelling places, awakened desire for the "more" of life is not a sudden escape from pain. If we seek to escape from our various hells of addiction, attachments, and self-preoccupation simply to be free from pain, inevitably we remain stuck. We can emerge from this dwelling place only by accepting another kind of suffering, a suffering in union with Christ that is purifying and strengthening, instead of destructive and meaningless. Meaningless pain may bring a person into therapy, but if the need for moral conversion is not addressed, cure on a more superficial level of the self may seem to take place, but inner healing will not happen. Issues in need of healing will reassert themselves. Here, most distractions in prayer probably come from specific areas of un-freedom that tempt us to relapse. Experiences of addiction or infatuation, where one's thoughts compulsively focus around the desired person or object, are second dwelling place experiences where understandably, as Teresa says, the person tends to rise and fall. She repeats with frequency the need for *determination* to be for God and that we work and prepare ourselves with *determination* and make every possible effort to bring our will into conformity with God's will (II.1.8).[4]

---

[4]   Note Teresa's frequent reference to determination in chapter 11 of *The Book of Her Life*.

Today both light and darkness surround us. We find ourselves at the threshold of the post-modern world and already in
a new millennium. We experience radical cultural changes, and
we are witness to the birth of cultures and subcultures. A German sociologist, Gerhard Schulze, describes the German cultural
scene in a way that applies equally to us. He says that primacy
is given to "the aesthetic beauty of everyday life." The things of
everyday (clothes, entertainment, cars, leisure) are organized in
such a way that everything is wrapped with the quality of ad-
venture, so as to provoke pleasant sensations. Behind these de-
velopments there is, on the one hand, the sensation of life as
being strongly individualistic; and on the other, when confronting oneself with others, the tendency toward a sense of security
that acts according to the motto, "relationships without ties."
Immediate experience, image and sensation, become almost a
"secular religion."

Advertisements can be powerful sources of distraction. We
see a commercial on TV, or even more persuasive, on the Internet, and immediately desire for the object hooks us. We may
not need it and we may not be able to afford it, but it keeps in-
serting itself into our consciousness saying, "Buy me, buy me!"
We are all influenced in one way or another by our post-modern world. This is the age in which we live and which shapes
the struggle that is uniquely ours in coming to freedom for God.
We do not live in a vacuum. The meaning and promise of God
enfleshed in Christ Jesus is that God works through the human
condition as it shapes itself in every age. God will bring the soul
to the needed level of moral conversion and inner freedom
through its struggles with the distracting enticements of the
senses. Moral conversion effects the beginning of a long process
by which God educates human desire through God's self-revelatory process in the depth of the soul so that desire for worldly
values and desire for God are no longer in conflict. Distractions

in the second dwelling places point to the need for moral conversion away from a dissipated life (II.1.9). Teresa concludes her discussion of these dwelling places with a reminder of the importance of good spiritual guidance along with the need for prayer and a reflective life that deepens self-knowledge and awakens love for Christ (II.1.10-11). Such practices, in spite of continued inner conflict, prepare the soul to venture into the third dwelling places.

CHAPTER THREE

THE THIRD DWELLING PLACES

Persons in the third dwelling places, over a period of time have turned away from sin and are trying to live a life pleasing to God. Because they have straightened out their lives through moral conversion and the practice of virtue, they tend to think they have arrived. Self-satisfied complacency easily takes hold. Various descriptions of such persons lead one to see the third dwelling places as the area of potential ego inflation. Aware of this temptation, Teresa begins her account of these dwelling places with lengthy and cogent reflections against false security. This may be a time of spiritual fervor but it is not the end of the journey. Teresa exhorts her daughters with passion: "Enter, enter, my daughters into the interior rooms, pass on from your little works" (III.1.6). One senses her exasperation at those who make an issue of a little dryness in prayer as she exhorts her reader to humility (II.1.7; III.1.9).

These third dwelling places are important since "there are many persons in the world who arrive here and their virtues are many." As Teresa says:

> They long not to offend His Majesty, even guarding themselves against venial sins; they are fond of doing penance and setting aside periods of recollection; they

spend their time well, practicing works of charity toward their neighbors; and are very balanced in their use of speech and dress and in governing of their households. (III.1.5).

Admirable as this may sound, the problem is that the third dwelling places can best be described as "settling in for less." Persons easily become complacent, too comfortable with what is, and subsequently they become closed to deeper realities. Everything is well ordered and under control, including God. New ideas that threaten this room of false security, but which could lead to a deeper, fuller life in God, are shut out. For her nuns Teresa describes it this way: "We seem to think that everything is done when we willingly take and wear the religious habit and abandon all worldly things and possessions for Him" (II.1.8). When we have settled in for less, anything beyond one's way of seeing things appears threatening since it beckons us to stretch to a changed vision of reality. New biblical or theological insights often find a cold reception in this dwelling place. Here, persons tend to cling to *their way* of seeing things as *the only way. Clinging* to rigid conservative **or** rigid liberal views, without openness to other ways of seeing things, is a struggle with third dwelling place distractions.[1]

Usually third dwelling place distractions have to do with others and their failure, real or imagined, to meet our expectations. Critical thoughts, putting others down, or putting oneself down, are third dwelling place distractions. Many influences shape our values and the things we hold dear. The point here is not that we be without values, but that we remain open to un-

---

[1] I found it interesting that a very fine priest with a good liturgical sense so reacted to a lector who read from the Missalette, instead of from the Lectionary, that he stayed angry over the issue for weeks.

derstanding the values that others hold, even though we choose to remain firm in our own. Unfortunately, as Teresa points out, our perfect and settled self and the beliefs we hold, become a standard for judging others who inevitably fall short. Teresa wisely admonishes: "Let us look at our own faults and leave aside those of others, for it is very characteristic of persons with such well ordered lives to be shocked by everything. What is most lacking in the third dwelling place is humility" (III.2.13). Probably from experience, Teresa observes that it is useless to give such persons advice because since they have engaged so long in the practice of virtue they think they can teach others. They feel more than justified in being disturbed should God try them in some minor matter (III.2.1). Dryness in prayer becomes an affront, and adversities in life cause inordinate disturbance and affliction (III.2.1-2). Teresa tells of the rich man with a surplus of wealth who worries over a small financial loss as if he would not have a piece of bread left to nourish his hunger (III.2.4). Disturbing distractions centering on fear of loss, especially when the matter is not significant — small financial losses, loss of a little honor, loss of health, loss of happiness and delight in God — mark this dwelling place (III.2.4,5,8,9). Temptations in these dwelling places seem to be toward perpetual feasting on negativity bolstered by feelings of self-righteousness.

Furthermore, consonant with the somewhat narcissistic, judgmental attitude that Teresa describes, a person's image of God tends also to be rigid and to bear the confusion of projection, displacement, idealization or self-devaluation. In projection, a person's thoughts become God's thoughts; *God* "thinks the way I do," whereas Teresa would have us be truly attentive to the will of God (III.2.6). In displacement, God becomes the angry or rejecting parent or someone else of one's experience. When God tries them in some minor matter they go about disturbed and afflicted (III.2.1). An idealized God is often the cuddly god who will not allow bad things to happen to us — like dryness in prayer (III.1.7). When we project our self-devaluation onto God, it becomes impossible to believe in God's love because we are so hateful in our own eyes. As Teresa has it, persons canonize their feelings of wretchedness instead of letting them be beneficial for humility (III.2.2,3).

Ana-Maria Rizzuto writes about this dynamic in her book, *The Birth of the Living God*.[2] She attempts to bring together a comprehensive theory of the origins, evolution, and significance of the god representation in psychic life. Her study reveals the ingenuity of the child in creating a god representation through experience and fantasy. Like the transitional object, God is heavily loaded with parental traits. Rizzuto says that the first time a child enters a church or synagogue he or she already has their pet god under their arm. It is important for those who do religious instruction with children to find out what this pet god looks like.

Images of God tell us about ourselves. Rizzuto illustrates how such images develop out of psychic experience. In her research, clients' drawings of God have such titles as: *God, the enigma* and *God, my enemy*. Through case histories she identifies these images as projections of parental and family relationships. Projections of God reflect attitudes toward life. The woman who drew the picture entitled *God, my enemy* felt that, from childhood on, everyone hated her, and she had good reason to think so, considering the hurts and tragedies of her childhood experience.

The third dwelling places invite exploration of one's God image. They also invite us beyond the world of immediacy — beyond sense satisfaction where we rest complacent in good feel-

---

2   Ana-Maria Rizzuto, M.D., *The Birth of the Living God: A Psychoanalytic Study* (Chicago, IL: University of Chicago Press, 1981).

ings especially at prayer, beyond over-reliance on sense informa-tion, beyond over-security in our beliefs — to a world mediated by deeper meaning. God invites us to what Bernard Lonergan calls intellectual conversion. The third dwelling places invite us to humility through an intellectual conversion that opens doors to deeper levels of meaning informed by gospel values. We need such a conversion if we are to respond to the invitation of the other dwelling places where self-transcendence leads one further into the mystery of God and into the ambiguities of human life. Our person is being opened to God and to that which in the end matters most in life. We are being drawn beyond worldly suc-cess as the basis of our identity, beyond superficial religion, through intellectual conversion to a deeper reality: religious con-version or, as Lonergan puts it — to otherworldly falling in love.[3]

Grace works in the third dwelling places through experi-ences of disillusionment and dryness in prayer. Here, *disillusion-ment is grace*. It invites us beyond sense satisfaction, beyond the rational and the immediate toward contemplative understand-ing. In contemplative prayer, it is *God* who unlocks the doors of reason and invites the soul beyond, into regions deeper than the rational mind can penetrate. The self, stripped of its illusions, its grandiosity, and the defenses of the false self, is further pre-pared to travel on to the place where "the soul gives to God, God himself in God" (LF 3.78); where in the inner wine cellar of the heart, Martha and Mary join together in serving the Lord (VII.4.12).

As Teresa repeatedly affirms, significant to these third dwelling places, is growth in self-knowledge. Her descriptions of the issues these dwellers struggle with sound like those issues we recognize today as involving the narcissistically injured per-

---

[3] Lonergan, *Method in Theology*, p. 240.

sonality. Given human finite fragility overshadowed by original sin, none of us escapes being at least tainted with narcissism. Full blown, narcissism cuts short one's potential for genuine relatedness, and therefore for genuine humanity. Distractions that characterize the third dwelling places, as Teresa describes them, all reflect some narcissistic enmeshment. She advises that we seek out someone who is free from illusion about the things of the world (III.2.12). Today persons in these dwelling places might benefit from appropriate forms of psychotherapy. This could help them toward the inner freedom needed for intimate relationship with others, including a relationship with God. Narcissism, even in small doses, minimizes a person's potential for intimacy. Psychotherapy and spiritual guidance easily complement one another to help bring to consciousness defenses against relatedness. With help, we can learn to be in touch with and attentive to recurring distractions in the mind, and also with the feelings in the body inevitably triggered by our thoughts, imaginings, and attitudes. The body gives these a voice through our emotions. By listening to our body and to the feeling messages it gives, which we might prefer to deny, the meaning of distracting thoughts, and their invitation to conversion and transformation, can become clear. Attentiveness to feelings offers a powerful lesson in self-knowledge, which, as Teresa reminds us, is an essential preparation if we are to respond to God's invitation into the fourth dwelling places. Learning to identify shifts in the body that identify emotions can be realized without at the same time blaming or criticizing ourselves for having such feelings.[4] Each distraction creates its own corresponding emotion. Emotions themselves are a form of distraction. Strong

---

[4] Eugene Gendlin, Ph.D., offers valuable techniques of self-therapy that teach persons how to identify and change the way personal problems concretely exist in the body. See: *Focusing* (New York: Bantam Books, revised edition, 1981).

emotions bind the mind so that rational thought becomes difficult or impossible. Instead, irrational wanderings, probably connected with whatever triggered the emotions, take over. In extreme cases, this becomes mental illness.

Like all classics the *Interior Castle* opens itself fully to those who return to it often. A single reading rarely discloses the full depth of its meaning. As I read and reread Teresa's accounts of the dwelling places, her insights appear increasingly significant for spiritual growth. Third dwelling place distractions can plague us through life, although the hold they have on us lessens as love increasingly overwhelms reason and teaches the wisdom of surrender (III.2.7). Growth in humility so essential to these third dwelling places (III.2.8-9), is also a lifetime process. Freedom from worry over health (III.2.8), attachment to one's own will, illusions about things of the world, lack of fortitude in suffering (III.2.12), and especially, difficulty in looking at our own faults and leaving aside those of others (III.2.13), ultimately is God's work. Different from fourth dwelling place distractions, in the third dwelling places, distractions in prayer need to be listened to and dealt with, for God speaks to us through them inviting an ever deeper conversion of heart and a less self-centered love in our relationship with God and others.

Third dwelling place distractions remind us that God is not finished with us yet. At the same time, their intrusion into a more mature phase of our spiritual journey might leave us feeling like we are backsliding, when in fact God is integrating growth that has already taken place into grace and growth presently in process. The insights that third dwelling place distractions offer can now be listened to with greater intellectual honesty. We can relate to them from the perspective of a deeper love, greater inner freedom, and greater sensitivity before God to all that displeases God. The pain at seeing oneself still so imperfect offers occasion for deepened humility and surrender to God's merciful love. This is a different response from the self-righteous denial characteristic of the third dwelling places. In these third dwelling places, a too narrow concept of God and subsequently of the self, minimizes the soul's capacity for self-surrender to God so essential for the passage into the fourth dwelling places and it also minimizes the person's ability to be for others in self-giving love.

Those engaged in spiritual guidance can discern the difference between a person in the third dwelling places and those who suffer third dwelling place distractions that reappear in the prayer and life of seasoned pray-ers by the intellectual honesty with which such distractions are acknowledged and owned. Growth in humility characterizes the journey deeper into the dwelling places. This means a person recognizes and accepts and even befriends the dark side of their person. The sin that is in us is not denied but rather its appearance finds a welcome because we have discovered God's caring presence even in that which is antithetical to God. God is present to our darkness. Here, all that is not of God becomes matter for God's purifying fire to take hold of and to transform into God-likeness through the humility, trust, and confidence in God its acceptance engenders. The intimate presence of Christ's risen transforming life to our darkness will be treated at length in the sixth dwelling places. As we begin to reflect on the fourth dwelling places we again recall Teresa's insistence that the journey through the castle is not a linear movement. We move in and out of the castle's myriad of rooms even though our deeper self continues to journey inward.

CHAPTER FOUR

THE FOURTH DWELLING PLACES

Letting go of control and learning surrender characterize the fourth dwelling places. In our prayer, God invites us beyond thought, beyond the merely rational to a deeper love and a more comprehensive surrender (IV.1.6). What Teresa names supernatural experiences begin here as we come closer to the center room where the King dwells — something Teresa finds difficult to explain (IV.1.1). Allowing that God's initiative is integral to all prayer, the fourth dwelling places focus on God's part in the conversation that is prayer. Here prayer takes place at a level deeper than the mind can grasp. Our psyche — in traditional language, the faculties of the soul — enters into a process of conditioning to receive the unique inflow of God that is contemplative prayer. Through faith, hope, and love, which constitute the dynamic of our relationship with God, God purifies our too narrow understanding both of God and of the self as God draws the soul into inner stillness. Initially the result might feel more like inner chaos. "Terrible trials are suffered because we don't understand ourselves and that which isn't bad at all but good we think a serious fault," laments Teresa (IV.1.9). We are not yet at home in the world of the spirit so the chaos of the mind causes great affliction. For as Teresa earlier reminded us:

Just as we cannot stop the movement of the heavens, so neither can we stop our mind; and then the faculties of the soul go with it, and we think we are lost and have wasted the time spent before God. But the soul is perhaps completely joined with him in the dwelling places very close to the center while the mind is on the outskirts of the castle suffering from a thousand wild and poisonous beasts and meriting by this suffering. As a result we should not be disturbed: nor should we abandon prayer, which is what the devil wants us to do (IV.1.9).

Because this prayer "is like the flowing spring in which the water does not come through aqueducts — the soul restrains itself or is restrained in its realization that it doesn't understand what it desires; and so the mind wanders from one extreme to the other, like a fool unable to rest in anything" (IV.3.8). At the same time, all the turmoil in her head, which Teresa describes in IV.1.10, doesn't hinder prayer. Rather, "the soul is completely taken up in its quiet, love, desire, and clear knowledge." God is taking a more active part in our prayer but at a depth beyond the mind's comprehension. This creates disturbance since as Teresa says, "the mind is on the outskirts of the castle." On the level of the mind, the face of God is frequently clouded over by the mind's projections as to **who** God is, and with expectations as to **how** God should respond to our initiatives. The God of incomprehensible mystery invites the soul to surrender preconceived notions of God and to rest in the dark quiet of a perhaps barely perceived presence. Our need to control what happens in prayer is also being purified and led to surrender. In this transitional time, "it isn't good for us to be disturbed by our thoughts, nor should we be concerned, but simply endure them for the love of God" (IV.1.11).

Something new is happening in our relationship with God. God is taking a specific initiative in our prayer through a silent inflow of loving knowledge. Since the mind is as yet unconditioned for God it reacts with confusion to a conversation that takes place in silence. Our thoughts roam about in the outskirts of the castle while, as Teresa reminds us, "the soul is perhaps completely joined with God in the dwelling places very close to the center" (IV.1.9).

Distractions have a different meaning in the fourth dwelling places. All prayer is at the initiative of God's indwelling Spirit. Something unique, however, happens in this form of prayer. It is the beginning of what is traditionally known as infused contemplation. This unique inflow of God's Trinitarian life calls for a unique response in regard to distractions. In these dwelling places for the most part, distractions are to be endured not dealt with, at least during the time of prayer.

"A brilliantly shining beautiful castle" (I.2.1), is only one of many images that Teresa uses in her effort to describe the dynamic of the soul's life in God. She likens it to "a pearl from the Orient, a tree of life planted in the very living waters of life — that is, in God" (I.2.1). I find that the biblical image of the tree is one way of giving symbolic expression to the movement through the first three dwelling places into the rooms of contemplative prayer. A tree through its leaves draws life from the sun while the roots absorb moisture from the earth. All the forces of nature interact with the tree to strengthen, make beautiful or distort its shape, or possibly through nature's violence, to completely uproot it. The sap, the life force of the tree, flows through the trunk and into the branches. External elements affect the tree but it also depends on the soil below for moisture and nourishment. Its roots extend ever deeper into the soil as it grows in height and through its roots, the tree draws into itself many nutrients essential to its life.

Prayer in the first three dwelling places is like the outer life of a tree. It engages various facets of what the Harvard psychologist Charles Verge calls "the contextual self." The contextual self comprises the narrow confines of the ego and the dimensions of our person bound by conditions of time and space such as body, psyche, emotions and all the dimensions of our person that are contingent and permeable. The activity of the contextual self is essential to us as human beings and through it we can grow in our life with God. Vocal prayer, meditation techniques, use of scripture, the rosary, centering prayer, or what Teresa would call the prayer of recollection, are all ways by which in faith the contextual self reaches out to God.

Along with the contextual self is what Verge calls "the divine self." The divine self is that place of unconditional acceptance within which the human and the divine encounter each other.[1] This process of encounter assumes special meaning in the fourth dwelling places. As we reach out to God through our human effort, simultaneously is God reaching out to us just as the sap of the tree, and the nutrients from the soil, make their way through the trunk of the tree to nourish the life of the branches, and allow the tree to bud and blossom. Our reaching for God and God reaching for us interact in the fourth dwelling places. Without effort on our part, the divine presence within quietly makes itself known. God's mysterious, subtle touch penetrates human consciousness. This happens in a manner no longer dependent on information from the contextual self. The senses are not involved in this process. Teresa describes it well in giving us the difference between consolation and spiritual delights. Consolation is the normal human response to joyful or pleasant expe-

---

[1] Charles Verge, Ph.D., "Foundations for a Spiritually Based Psychotherapy," in *Religion and Family*, edited by L. Burton (Hayworth Press, 1992), p. 40.

riences on the level of the contextual self while spiritual delight is the overflow of God's intimate presence in the depth of the divine self.

> Well now, in speaking about what I said I'd mention here concerning the difference in prayer between consolations and spiritual delights, the term "consolations," I think, can be given to those experiences we ourselves acquire through our own meditation and petitions to the Lord, those that proceed from our own nature — although God in the end does have a hand in them; for it must be understood, in whatever I say, that without Him we can do nothing. But the consolations arise from the virtuous work itself that we perform, and it seems that we have earned them through our own effort and are rightly consoled for having engaged in such deeds (IV.1.4).

Teresa considers it important that we understand the difference between consolations that begin in our human nature, and which are natural to our reaching out to God and the spiritual delights that come directly from God in the depth of the soul and then find their way into conscious awareness as a kind of divine overflow (IV.1.4-6).

> The spiritual delights begin in God, but human nature feels and enjoys them as much as it does those I mentioned — and much more (IV.1.4).[2]

---

2 Another of Teresa's examples that illustrates the functioning of the contextual and the divine self as it relates to prayer is found in IV.2.2-6.

She reminds us that she has spoken at length on this subject elsewhere.[3] Consolations, which are the fruit of our reaching out to God, often have the self-satisfied characteristics of third dwelling place experiences.

> But the consolations arise from the virtuous work itself that we perform, and it seem that *we have earned them through our own effort and are rightly consoled* for having engaged in such deeds (IV.1.4). (Emphasis mine)

With psychological astuteness, Teresa remarks that the same consolation can come from human endeavors that are pleasing like suddenly inheriting a great fortune or success in a business matter (IV.1.4). Consolations are the human response to what is pleasing whether it be in relation to God or to any human experience. As Teresa observes, "For the most part, the souls in the previous dwelling places are the ones who have these devout feelings for these souls work almost continually with the intellect, engaging in discursive thought and meditation" (IV.1.6).

Distracting thoughts around feelings of consolation or their absence test whether these bear the fruits of humility, often lacking in the third dwelling places (IV.1.6). Persistent feelings of self-pity or resentment that consolations are few or wanting alert us to pray for the gift of humility. This is not an exercise in self-depreciation but rather, as Teresa reminds us: humility is truth. To walk in truth is to realize both our giftedness and our human fragility. Fragile creatures that we are however, our awe-

---

[3] See *The Book of Her Life*, chapter 12. Here Teresa continues her development of prayer under the image of four ways of watering a garden. Also see: *The Way of Perfection*, pp. 16-25, which deals with the beginnings of contemplative prayer.

some reality is that the God of incomprehensible mystery loves us and invites us to an intimate relationship. Humility is the fruit of such genuine self-knowledge that recognizes the complexity of the human before God. Humility enables fragile humanity to feel at home with God.[4] Self-knowledge gained through psychotherapy or other means does not necessarily lead to humility, whereas growth in self-knowledge through prayer always goes hand-in-hand with growth in humility. Genuine humility is always grounded in human/God relatedness.

Throughout her writings, Teresa contends with what she considers her lack of self-understanding. In IV.1.7-11 she draws us into her struggle to understand the difference between the imagination (or the mind, as she calls it) and the intellect. Her efforts to unravel the difference between the two bring us back to the image of the tree. At winter's end, the sap circulates again through the trunk of the tree to the tightly covered winter-protected buds. The buds need to surrender their protective covering if they are to swell and open out into new growth. Likewise, in what Teresa calls *the prayer of quiet*, God invites us to surrender human activity and to let our soul expand as the divine energies of the Spirit flow from the center room into the faculties of the soul. God invites the contextual self — the body/psyche complex with its limited view of reality — beyond its narrow confines, through *surrender*, to a deeper reality. Sometimes the contextual self seems glad to give way to this new reality so the soul settles into a place of quiet absorption in God. At other times it may react to the quiet, being more comfortable within the confusion of earlier dwelling places. In this case, Teresa observes that "the soul suffers from a thousand wild and poisonous beasts,"

---

[4] See my study of humility in Teresa's writings: "Teresa Revisions Humility: A Matter of Justice," found in *The Land of Carmel* (Roma: Institutum Carmelitanum, Via Sforza Pallavicini 10, 1991), pp. 337-346.

but adds for our encouragement, "while it merits from such suffering."

If this is happening in our prayer, "we should not be disturbed nor should we abandon prayer, which is what the devil wants us to do" (IV.1.9). From personal experience Teresa offers wise counsel: that in the fourth dwelling places we are not to be disturbed by our thoughts nor should we be concerned by the mind's rebellious reaction to the initial dynamic of contemplative prayer, *the prayer of quiet* (IV.1.11). With prudent sagaciousness she advises us not to demand consolation in prayer and not to take over God's part in the conversation by human effort. When the mind is free — that is, not absorbed by the divine presence — do all that you can to help yourself, especially when the mind wanders and prayer is dry. The soul is learning humility, receptivity, and self-knowledge. "Let us recognize our misery...."

> But that we desire to rest from the thousand trials there are in the world and that the Lord wants to prepare us for tranquility and that within ourselves lies the obstacle to such rest and tranquility cannot fail to be very painful and almost unbearable. So let the Lord bring us to the place where these miseries will not taunt us, for they seem sometimes to be making fun of the soul (IV.1.12).

We cannot reach God through the pure grit of human effort. Surrender is the key to entering that inner space of tranquility unreachable through human effort and which is outside of the realm of self-made images of God constructed of our own needs and desires. For this reason the fourth dwelling places are necessarily characterized by letting go of control and learning surrender. From this experience usually issues another important insight. Just as prayer and the wanderings of the mind cannot be controlled, neither can the rest of life be controlled. In the process of surrender, our relationship to the rest of reality changes. In human relationships, we begin to let persons be. We have less need to control the lives of others or to take responsibility for their problems or shortcomings or to make them over, because being closer to the center room, the eyes of the soul begin to see the self and others through the eyes of God. In the fourth dwelling places a refocusing of how we perceive the whole of reality begins to happen. As the self becomes less self-centered by being more centered in God, the light of God illumines all that is human.[5] Thus Teresa can marvel at the grandeurs of God as God enlarges her heart and re-educates her spirit, in fact her whole person, for direct enjoyment of God without created intervention. What is physical or of the senses, receives the overflow of God's self-communication in the spirit (IV.2.5-6).

The earlier dwelling places involve the normal human processes of interiority. We realize self-possession as we become aware, intelligent, critical and responsible.[6] In the fourth dwelling places we learn, often through dryness in prayer, what it is to love beyond the lure of feeling and even thought. The Divine within continually invites a deeper love and a deeper surrender. We learn that life cannot be controlled. Most of all, as we begin to encounter the absolute "otherness" of God, we learn not to take God for granted, and not to squeeze God into our too narrow concepts.[7] Therefore, every invitation to transcendence, to letting go of control into a deeper spiritual awareness where one

---

[5] See DN 2.1-3.

[6] See *Method*, p. 13 ff.

[7] The Book of Job has it right. God cannot be encapsulated in the formulas of the Eliphazes, Bildads and Zophars symbolized in our too narrow thinking either about God, ourselves, others, the Church or the universe.

is less imprisoned in the petty, oversensitive, personal world of the ego, into participation in the wider world of God and the universe, I suggest, is a fourth dwelling places experience.

The fourth dwelling places are transitional spaces where the experience of both intimacy and transcendence confronts selfish narcissism along with the residue of immature god-images. As we become receptive of God as loving mystery who both defies control and, at the same time, is intimate to all human activity, like a mirror, God — truth itself — reflects back the untruth of all that is inauthentic in the soul.[8] In this process, like a fruitful spring, God quietly waters the garden of the soul and charms the divine self, and at times even the contextual self, into stillness.[9]

So how do we deal with distractions in the fourth dwelling places? In IV.1.9, Teresa encourages us to recognize our miseries. When the lure of God in prayer leaves the desire to quietly rest in the silence of God, if we simply identify our "miseries" — what at this moment is disturbing our prayer — this *naming* not infrequently, results in at least the beginnings of inner quiet. To simply identify feelings such as anger, hurt, anxiety and restlessness, without analyzing the feelings, without judging ourselves for having such feelings, but simply recognizing that they are there by naming them, is important to letting the quiet of God find its way into the outer levels of the contextual self. When the heart is quiet, we can be more receptive to God's illumination. To leave feelings unnamed results in disquietude, which in turn allows distractions to control the mind. It is im-

---

[8] See Vilma Seelaus, "The Self: Mirror of God" in *The Way* (London, England: Heythrop College, July 1992), pp. 225-236.

[9] As already noted, Teresa uses the image of two founts with two water troughs to explain the effects of contemplative prayer as different from human effort. IV. 2.2-6.

portant to remember that distractions are one way through which feelings make themselves known.

Naming our feelings allows God to shed light on our inner darkness. We might discover that under our anger is a persistent urge to control the life of another/other persons, or that we still cling to unresolved resentments over past hurts or losses. We might discover over-sensitivity to criticism; things that we are attached to might appear to stare us in the face; addictions that block the flow of living water and cause problems in family or in our work might confront us with the truth of their presence. I am convinced that under every persistent distraction there exists both a feeling to be named and a deeper issue to be confronted and exposed for God's healing and transformation. A quiet mind helps us to be aware of what is going on in the body, in our feelings, in the heart, and in the world around us. A peaceful heart is a welcoming environment wherein God's silence loves to dwell.

In chapter three of her discussion of the fourth dwelling places Teresa nuances the soul's journey into contemplative prayer. The experience begins with what she calls the prayer of recollection, "which the Lord gives for the most part before the prayer of quiet." This chapter contains valuable advice in regard to distractions. In Teresa's imagery, the people of the castle — senses and faculties — are now more willing to stay close to the castle having wandered for years outside its walls, "even though they may not manage to remain inside because the habit of doing so is difficult to acquire. But still, they are not traitors...." She then uses the comparison of a shepherd whose barely perceptible whistle has such power that the faculties abandon exterior things and enter the castle (IV.3.2). "One notably senses a gentle drawing inward..." which Teresa then compares to a hedgehog curling up or a turtle drawing into its shell (IV.3.3). What she says next is significant. Teresa takes exception to books of her day that advise the person in this state not to engage in discourse, but to remain attentive and aware of what the Lord is working in it. Teresa disagrees and she finds support for her position in "the saintly Friar Peter of Alcantara... he says the same thing I do; although not in my words" (IV.3.4). She then shores up her argument with four significant points. First, the soul does become quite a fool when it tries to induce this prayer, and it is left much drier; and the imagination perhaps becomes more restless through the effort made not to think of anything. Her second reason is that these interior works are all gentle and peaceful. Doing something arduous would cause more harm than good. The example she gives of something arduous is holding one's breath to induce prayer. Third, the very care used not to think of anything will perhaps rouse the mind to think very much. Her fourth point is a reminder that prayer is not for our comfort and delight, but for the honor and glory of God. In this prayer we do what we can to cut down the rambling of the intellect — but not suspend either it or the mind (IV.3.5-7). She insists that in this prayer of recollection, meditation, or the work of the intellect, must not be set aside although it should be gentle so as not to hinder the divine activity beginning to shape the soul for contemplative prayer.[10]

John of the Cross gives three signs which indicate the beginnings of contemplative prayer. The *first* sign is the realization that one cannot make discursive meditation nor receive satisfaction from it as before. Dryness is usually the outcome. The *second* sign is an awareness of the disinclination to fix the imagination or sense faculties upon other particular objects, interior or exterior. "I am not affirming that the imagination will not come and go (even in deep recollection it usually wanders freely) but that the person is disinclined to fix it purposely upon extrane-

---

[10] See also WP 26.1 where Teresa explains a method for recollecting one's mind.

ous things." The *third* and surest sign is that a person likes to remain alone in loving awareness of God, without particular considerations, in interior peace and quiet and repose, and without the acts and exercises (at least discursive — those in which one progresses point by point) of intellect, memory and will, and that he/she prefers to remain alone in general, loving awareness and knowledge we mentioned, without any particular knowledge or understanding.[11]

In this experience, the use of a mantra as is used in centering prayer, can actually get in the way of a deeper reality.[12] The soul feels as if the words, or even a single word, choke the soul. The eyes spontaneously close. This initial experience of contemplative prayer can also be one of great dryness where nothing seems to be happening even though the soul is drawn to prayer. Within this desert of sense-deprivation, the mind wanders in search of an oasis of relief. Teresa advises that we not go after the mind in its wanderings when the fire of God seems to be dying embers, but gently to throw a straw of love in hope of enkindling the fire and regaining interior recollection. Again, in regard to distractions, we simply note them and let them go.

Experiences of dryness and sense-deprivation in prayer help to condition the soul/psyche for God. Although God-related by nature, the contextual self needs to be conditioned for deeper experiences of God through surrender. Our psyche in particular awaits the conditioning of the theological virtues of faith, hope, and love so that our knowing, our understanding, and our desiring become rooted in God and alive with the movement of God's Holy Spirit. John of the Cross reminds us that faith is the only proximate and proportionate means for union with God.

---

[11] See John of the Cross A2.13.2-4; DN 1.9.1-6; also WP 30.3-5; 31.12.

[12] See the writings of Thomas Keating and the many books available on centering prayer.

At this stage of the prayer journey we are still too much within the human mode of functioning in prayer. Our access to God through faith, hope, and love needs the strengthening of practice. Faith in particular needs to be exercised. Dryness in the fourth dwelling places is not from attachment to created realities as in earlier dwelling places; rather, it is the effect of the psyche's inability to cope with the silent inflow of God. God is making room for God. Just as fast moving waters hollow out a place for themselves and shape their path, so too does the inflow of God increasingly shape us into the divine likeness so that we too become fluid before God in complete surrender.

Since the experience is beyond human comprehension, it might seem that nothing is happening in our prayer except for a subtle *something* that draws us to prayer in spite of the dryness. The appropriate response is one of receptive faith. Although it seems as if nothing is happening, in fact, our soul is being conditioned to receive more of God. Teresa offers excellent advice in the fourth dwelling places regarding distractions. We are not to think much but to love much and so do that which best stirs us to love because love does not consist in great delight but in desiring with strong determination to please God in everything and to desire the things of God. "Don't think the matter lies in thinking of nothing else, and that if you become a little distracted all is lost" (IV.1.7-14).

Most persons serious about prayer have some experience of the fourth dwelling places. With it usually comes a compelling need for greater simplicity and a more contemplative way of life. This inner urgency toward simplicity and a less hurried lifestyle is sometimes confused with a call to contemplative life within an established contemplative Order. Frenetic living inevitably breeds distractions in prayer. The prayer of quiet stirs desire for more quiet in everyday life. If we listen to the voice of our distractions, these will alert us to steps that need to be taken for our inner and outer lives to be more consonant one with each other. Not just times of retreat are important here, but a general retreat from sterile busyness that simply feeds the ego with a sense of self-importance.

Some time ago I was struck by the words of St. Ambrose in a treatise found in the Liturgy of the Hours that show the interrelatedness between prayer and life. He writes:

> Again, Christ urges you, when you ask forgiveness for yourself, to be especially generous to others, so that your actions may commend your prayer. As the Apostle, too, teaches you how to pray: you must avoid anger and contentiousness, so that your prayer may be serene and wholesome. He tells you also that every place is a place of prayer, though our Savior says, "Go into your room."
>
> By the "room" you must understand, not a room enclosed by walls that imprison your body, but the room that is within you, that room where you hide your thoughts, where you keep your affections. This room of prayer is always with you, wherever you are, and it is always a secret room, where only God can see you.[13]

I suggest that this inner room of prayer is the reality of Christ's abiding presence. In the fourth dwelling places the energies of the Risen Christ draw us into the enclosed room of prayer in order to entice the soul into the expansiveness of God. The energies of Christ are relational/Trinitarian energies that purify the private self of its illusion that such a thing as a *private self* can

---

[13] See *The Liturgy of the Hours*, Volume Four (New York: Catholic Book Publishing Co., 1975), p. 347.

actually exist. We are like the Trinity: of and for one another. In the fourth dwelling places, Christ begins to take hold of the dis-ordered energy at work in the human soul — that gravitational pull toward self-centeredness — and channels it into Trinitarian Love, which is fully realized in the seventh dwelling places.

CHAPTER FIVE

THE FIFTH DWELLING PLACES

In the fifth dwelling places God invites the soul into its deepest center through touches of divine union. These experiences of union with God, however brief, cultivate the growth of self-surrender, and deepen in the soul the roots of abandonment to God, a process initiated in the fourth dwelling places. That God wants everything for God becomes increasingly clear to the soul in these fifth dwelling places (V.1.3). Here we begin to glimpse the full possibility of what we humans are created to be. In these dwelling places, God gives the grace to move beyond vestiges of self-centered living, to a continually deepened self-surrender of the soul to God. Desires that motivate us toward the good are now being completely centered in God as the soul is united with God in prayer. Says Teresa: "All their desires are directed toward pleasing You" (V.1.1). To keep us from illusion, Teresa makes clear that union with God has practical implications:

> ...One has to strive to go forward in the service of the Lord and in self-knowledge (V.3.1). True union can very well be reached with God's help if we make the effort to obtain it by keeping our will fixed only on that which is God's will (V.3.3).

Keeping the will fixed on that which is God's will leads the soul into loving surrender of its own purely ego agenda, that which Teresa names self-love and self-will. Essential to such surrender is growth in self-knowledge through which we come to recognize the stirrings of self-love. Distractions in these dwelling places help toward such recognition, as we shall explore further on. When Teresa deals with what she calls "supernatural prayer" — prayer initiated by God — distractions serve as invitations to a depth of self-knowledge that takes us beyond superficial self-awareness. To be in touch with what is deep within through self-knowledge helps us to identify stirrings of self-love, subtle movements toward ego inflation, and whatever else contaminates total being for God.

Psychology stresses the importance of self-possession for full human development. Jung claims that it is the task of the first half of life. It finds particular expression in the first three dwelling places through the practice of prayer, and in efforts toward Christian living. In the normal growth process, one's identity takes shape through self-maintenance in the use of one's talents, and in achieving goals that we set for ourselves. We become self-affirming as we learn to make decisions and to undertake commitments that give direction to our life. We also become self-justifying; we learn to be less affected by what others think of us. Their stance of approval or disapproval does not prevent us from standing secure within our own values and beliefs. We can stand secure in the values we hold in the midst of opposing values.

This initially necessary, self-centered focus however, is not the end of the journey. Self-possession is easily tainted with "self-love and self-will." It can leave us with a superficial self-understanding based on real or imagined achievements described by Teresa in the third dwelling places. A sense of self, based on our achievements, is often realized at the expense of others. As we climb over our peers up the ladder of success, the temptation to consider ourselves better than others is seldom absent. When we cling to self-possession and resist the invitation to self-surrender, we can stay stuck within the imperatives of success, efficiency, or serving the power interests of others. Paradoxically, should this happen, our sense of self becomes increasingly fluid and tends to change according to each situation.[1] The self and the values it holds, shift with the expectations of others, or according to the coloring of each situation. Out of her culture and experience, where asserting one's rights was important to maintain honor, Teresa could write:

> We love ourselves very much; there's an extraordinary amount of prudence we use so as not to lose our rights (V.4.6).

The inner imperative toward self-surrender of the fifth dwelling places exposes attachments to self-possession as God draws the soul, through divine union, into the self-emptying God revealed in Christ. As Teresa insists, Jesus is always both our companion and our model in the journey toward union with God. Self-surrender is a door opening to deeper reaches of being, where through contemplation and union with God, the "divine self" comes to realize its infinite capacity for God. Teresa laments our tendency to too easily settle on the superficial, and on a self-definition based on achievement and success. Her challenging words are not without a tinge of sadness that we overlook so great a human potential for lesser realities. She writes:

---

[1] See "The Self in Postmodern Thought: A Carmelite Response" by Vilma Seelaus, OCD (*Review for Religious*, September-October 1999, Vol. 58), pp. 454-468.

Yet few of us dispose ourselves that the Lord may
communicate it (this precious pearl of contemplation)
to us. In exterior matters we are proceeding well so
that we will reach what is necessary; but in the practice of virtues that are necessary for arriving at this
point we need very, very much and cannot be care-
less in either small things or great (V.1.2).

Postmodern writers ponder this question of the human self
and its true identity. Emmanuel Levinas, a Jew, who suffered a
lengthy period of forced labor during the Nazi era in Europe,
came to the awareness that behind its facade of self-sufficiency
and control, the modern ego is a troubled creature, gnawed at
by an inescapable call which is "there" before it can even begin
to hide in the thickets of its own essence. The source of this call
is the infinite, which Levinas does not hesitate to refer to as God.

I do not come to be a subject by some judicious ma-
nipulation of my own ideas or circumstances. Rather,
whatever reality I have is coincident with the "trauma
of awakening," the inescapable calling of the Infinite
within my finitude in an "undergoing that no capacity comprehends" and which "devastates its site like a
devouring fire."[2]

In these fifth dwelling places, through repeated surrender,

---

[2] For an interesting overview of postmodern thought that stresses the importance
of self-surrender, see Mark McIntosh, *Mystical Theology: The Integrity of Spiritual-
ity and Theology* (Malden, MA: Blackwell Publishers, 1998), pp. 213-239. See also:
Emmanuel Levinas, *Otherwise than Being or Beyond Essence*, trans. Alphonso Lingis
(Dordrecht: Kluwer Academic Publishers, 1991), pp. 176-177. Also: *Powers and
Submissions: Spirituality, Philosophy and Gender*, by Sarah Coakley (Malden, MA:
Blackwell Publishers, 2002). Of particular note is the chapter entitled: "Kenosis
and Subversion," pp. 1-39.

the soul divests itself of self; it allows God, "through the trauma of awakening" (Levinas), to reconstruct the self into its true divine image. Distractions reveal false self-constructions which in due time will undergo the purifying fires of the sixth dwelling places. Paradoxically, divesting of self means that we pay more attention than ever to ourselves, as God, "like a devouring fire," lights up hidden corners and exposes within our finitude all that resists "the calling of the infinite," as Levinas puts it.

Experiences of union in the fifth dwelling places challenge the residue of superficial living. We are not to hold on to anything (V.1.3). Teresa wants us to understand that we are being invited into the secrets of God. The journey through the dwelling places is our response to God's abiding invitation to divine intimacy, to a living relationship of actual encounter with God. She finds no better analogy than that of human espousal and the intimacy of marriage, although she hastens to clarify that "the delights married people must experience are a thousand leagues distant."

> For it is all a matter of love united with love, and the actions of love are most pure and so extremely delicate and gentle that there is no way of explaining them, but the Lord knows how to make them very clearly felt (V.4.3).

Throughout the fifth dwelling places, Teresa focuses our thoughts on Christ. His relational identity with his *Abba* is our inspiration as we journey through the castle of life. Jesus found his whole identity in his union with, and surrender to, his Father's will. In the security of his particular relational identity with God, Jesus was without the need for self-maintenance, self-affirmation and self-justification. As the Dutch theologian Frans Jozef van Beeck writes:

His being-related to the Father makes him personally free and lends him a personal authority that amazes those around him. While living in total dependence on, total familiarity with, and total orientation to God, the man Jesus Christ is himself in a way no self-affirmation could ever hope to produce. This selfhood, however, is not an isolated selfhood, for Jesus' relationship to God precisely enables him to relate to others boundlessly. He is really there, present to others, in availability for an encounter that, while it animates the humblest gesture of outreach, knows no bounds.[3]

Jesus here mirrors the mysterious depth of each person's true identity. Like Jesus, ours is also a relational identity, rooted in God's Trinitarian life. Union with God, and with all things in God, is our ultimate fulfillment and the grounding of all genuine human encounter. This means that, like Jesus, we too can come to a depth of surrender that leaves us without the need to tenaciously hold on to an identity apart from God.

Distractions in these dwelling places have implications beyond the actual time of prayer. Their meaning and message is found in all that distracts us in daily living from the peace that issues from experiences of union with God. During the short time that the prayer of union lasts, distractions however, are not an issue:

There is no need here to use any technique to suspend the mind since all the faculties are asleep in this state

---

[3] For a profound and insightful development of Jesus' relational identity with God, see Frans Jozef van Beeck, SJ, *Christ Proclaimed: Christology as Rhetoric* (New York: Paulist Press, 1979). The chapter entitled "The Lamb Slain," pp. 401-463, is especially meaningful in relation to our own personal identity before God. It offers solid theological grounding for moving beyond self-maintenance, self-justification and self-affirmation, which is so limiting to the human spirit. The citation above is found on page 424.

— and truly asleep — to the things of the world and to ourselves. As a matter of fact, during the time that the union lasts the soul is left as though without its senses, for it has no power to think even if it wants to (V.1.4).

As humans, we are both knowers and lovers. In the experience of union, our senses, our psyche, the mind and intellect, instead of coming to knowledge and love through visible, material objects, here receive loving knowledge directly from God. God is communicating God's self to the soul. The faculties, says Teresa, become as if blind and deaf. They are spellbound by God. They enter into a deep quiet and repose beyond human effort and the soul is left with certitude of God's indwelling presence (V.1.9-11).

God pervades the inner and even the outer senses so that the eyes instinctively close. The awesomeness of God's embrace of the divine self in the depth of the soul overflows into conscious life and lures the contextual self into silence. Instead of functioning in the normal manner from stimuli gathered from the outer world through the senses, these outer dimensions of the self become as it were fascinated by God. While the experience of union lasts, God has the psyche's undivided attention. "There is neither imagination, nor memory, nor intellect that can impede this good" (V.1.5). Distractions momentarily shut down, or are so far on the edge of consciousness, that they are barely perceptible. They are however an issue to the extent that they affect us in daily living. Repeatedly Teresa assures us that the prayer of union implies union with the will of God. Such union is clearest and safest even though its full realization is not ours until we enter the seventh dwelling places (V.3.5).

Self-maintaining, self-affirming and self-justifying tendencies need to be completely transformed through repeated acts of surrender to the loving invitation of God's indwelling Spirit. Much in us still resists the absolute love of God and love of neighbor that characterizes union with the will of God (V.3.7). Unacknowledged, our self-serving tendencies are like the worm that gnawed away the ivy that shaded Jonah from the sun's searing rays (V.3.6).

> This happens through self-love, self-esteem, judging one's neighbors (even though in little things) a lack of charity for them, and not loving them as ourselves. For even though, while crawling along, we fulfill our obligation and no sin is committed, we don't advance very far in what is required for complete union with the will of God (V.3.6).

Union with God is all about love. God's love for us, and our responsive love, together enlarges our capacity to love as God loves. Love transforms us into God-likeness by which we move beyond self-concerns to loving others as God loves them — with God's own love. Teresa's summary of the fifth dwelling places bears repetition: *"All their desires are directed toward pleasing You"* (V.1.1). God's desires for us are clear: that we love God and love our neighbor. Distractions in these dwelling places alert us to self-centered concerns that inhibit love and cause disquiet of heart; whereas union with God results in "a very deep peace" (V.2.10). This peace is an abiding gift, the overflow of God's loving embrace, which increasingly deepens in the sixth and seventh dwelling places. Anything that disturbs or distracts us from this deep inner peace needs our attention. Particularly in the fifth dwelling places does God invite a recollected heart and mindfulness of God. God is like a hidden treasure. God strengthens the soul:

...that it may dig until it finds this hidden treasure. The truth is that the treasure lies within our very selves (V.1.2).

A person on a treasure hunt gives undivided attention to the task at hand. God has absolute claim on our attention. Having experienced the prayer of union, persons frequently make radical changes in their way of life in order to be more present, not only to God, but also to their own inner movements, for as Teresa alerts us, there are other unions than the union with God. "Even though these unions regard vain things, the devil will use such things to transport us when they are greatly loved" (V.1.6). I recall with amusement an experience in my teen years. As my latest male attraction proudly showed me his first car, he kept looking at it with sheer delight, repeating, "It's mine! It's all *mine!*" In an ecstasy of joy he was one with his car.

The union Teresa describes is above all such earthly joys, "...the difference is like that between feeling something on the rough outer covering of the body or in the marrow of the bones." Pleased with herself for the comparison, Teresa adds: "...and that was right on the mark, for I don't know how to say it better" (V.1.6). The prayer of union in the fifth dwelling places effects a different kind of consciousness from that of earthly joys. In the prayer of union, the energies of God's love penetrate from the roots of one's being through the essence of the soul. The snakes and lizards of the outer rooms of the castle cannot get into this inner space (V.1.5). While they cannot enter the inner space, they can however, distract, disturb, and disquiet — although not take away — our inner peace. These snakes and lizards appear in many shapes and sizes. In these dwelling places I suggest that they are whatever disturbs peace of heart and frazzles the mind. Our challenge is to be alert to the self-maintaining, self-affirming,

self-justifying tendencies invariably underneath such disturbances. Like stones and fallen trees in a running stream, self-
concerns block the flow of love from God, through us, to others.

Distractions here are more than thoughts that come and
go. Our emotions also distract us. Things like disquiet, anxiety,
fear, unrest, anger, etc., distract us from the realization of God's
inner peace. Such disquiet often points to basic attitudes toward
God, toward life and toward others that are not in harmony with
God's all-inclusive will to love. In these fifth dwelling places God
continually encourages us to lighten our grasp on self-concerns.
Self-concerns manifest themselves through the self-justifying dia-
logues that absorb the mind and disquiet the heart — perhaps
over a misunderstanding of small consequence. We need to notice our self-maintaining urge to straighten things out at the first
opportunity. Many things straighten themselves out without our
frenetic need to set the record straight. Much peace comes with
the ability to live with misunderstandings that, in the end, are
often inconsequential, but which offer insight for our personal
growth if we are open and honest before God and ourselves. By
listening to our disquiet of heart, and letting it lead us to deeper
levels of self-knowledge and of self-surrender, we save ourselves
from useless defensive reactions, and perhaps, from inflicting hurt
on others.

Surrender is not an abstract concept; it usually means something very specific, such as letting go of useless self-justification
as we become more secure in God's love. Things look different
in God's light. Our biased attitudes go through a process of transformation, which ultimately frees us of our self-justifying tendencies. Should the situation warrant it, we could then defend
ourselves, or our position, with a peaceful heart. Being in touch
with our own inner constraints widens our choices for response

(V.3.5-6). Unattended pervasive, distracting thoughts prevent us from being at peace within ourselves and from being a peaceful presence before others. Fortunately, we can learn from the wisdom of our distractions. Annoying, and sometimes painful distractions are a gift from deep within which can lead us to deeper levels of self-knowledge and inner freedom. In daily living, the process of learning immediate connection with our thoughts, and especially our feelings, can occasion prayerful moments as we turn to God's indwelling presence for help. The discomforts of our distractions are like labor pains. Our attachments and inner constraints are pushing for release. The chrysalis is ready to burst open so that the butterfly can emerge. Teresa cheers us on:

> Therefore, courage, my daughters! Let's be quick to do this work and weave this little cocoon by getting rid of our self-love and self-will, our attachments to any earthly thing.... (V.2.6).

Personal example

Teresa's reflections in these dwelling places have helped me to see how distractions play themselves out in my own life. When I find myself mentally going round and round a difficult or disturbing situation, or holding on to an emotion of anger, frustration, fear or self-pity, the way to recover my serenity is to take a minute to sit quietly in prayer. As I try truthfully to name what I am feeling, I ask God to let me see which of my potential self-destructive tendencies are gestating within my agitated mind, with the overflow of emotional reactions in my body. I consider my body to be my closest spiritual director. By way of its emotional reactions, it enables me to accurately name what is going on and to identify the more subliminal message of my distracting thoughts. I ask God to let me see beyond these disturbing thoughts and feelings to whatever in myself cries for a deeper surrender. Through years of entering into this process, most often I quickly recognize the residue of early life experiences that are contaminating the present situation. Once this reality is accurately named, the present situation comes into perspective, and I am enabled once again to surrender the hidden issues of my life story to God, and to embrace it as integral to my own inner transformation. Each time I am enabled to name in prayer that which binds me, I experience a deepened peace and freedom not only within, but also in regard to whatever the difficult or challenging situation at hand might be.

If anxiety over something is the genesis of a recurring distraction, in a quiet moment of prayer I might sense God reminding me that God is in control of the particular situation of distracting concern, so I can relax my intensity and let go of my impulse toward wanting to be in control. No matter the issue, it is not the end of the world. From this simple reminder of an easily forgotten truth, which issues in an attitudinal conversion, and as I relax in willing surrender, new perspectives tend to open up. I begin to see more sides of the situation as my critical mind gentles into more compassionate understanding. As I face my self-reliance (self-will) and my urge to set things right, I surrender myself, and the situation, to God. This process brings me again to a graced acceptance of my own dark side as well as that of others. Again, as this happens, I gain insight into the positive dimensions of this present trial toward spiritual transformation, as I surrender my darkness, into the flames of God's purifying love. Such experiences of surrender lighten the grip of attachments, and lead to inner peace. Experiences of ongoing attitudinal conversion and surrender to God what is not of God, are essential if we desire to journey further through the dwelling places to the center rooms.[4]

With the insight of experience, John of the Cross reminds us that

> Cares do not molest the detached, neither in prayer nor outside it. And thus losing no time, such people easily store up an abundance of spiritual good. Yet those who are attached spend all their time going to and fro about the snare to which their heart is tied, and even with effort they can hardly free themselves for a short while from the snare of thinking about and finding joy in the object to which their heart is attached.[5]

Our attachments create pleasurable thoughts, but they also contribute to the snares of recurring disturbing thoughts when we are faced with opposition, or with other difficult situations. When the heart is detached, problems will not go away, but they will cease to molest us. The difference between thoughts of genuine concern, and thoughts which are anchored somewhere in our ego-needs, is that these latter thoughts molest us, which is what distractions do. We feel molested and discomforted by them.[6]

---

[4] Bernard Lonergan in a chapter entitled "Self-Transcendence" echoes this reality. He writes: "As the question of God is implicit in all of our questioning, so being in love with God is the basic fulfillment of our conscious intentionality. That fulfillment brings a deep-set joy that can remain despite humiliation, failure, privations, pain, betrayal, desertion, etc. That fulfillment brings a radical peace, the peace that the world cannot give. That fulfillment bears fruit in a love of one's neighbor that strives mightily to bring about the kingdom of God on this earth. On the other hand, the absence of that fulfillment opens the way to the trivialization of human life in the pursuit of fun, to the harshness of human life arising from the ruthless absurd." From *Method in Theology* (New York: The Seabury Press, 1979), p. 105.

[5] *Ascent of Mount Carmel*, Book 3, p. 303.

[6] To feel molested conveys an unwanted experience although today it also has sexual connotations.

These uncomfortable feelings, however, are grace. God as it were, enters into the space of our attachments and agitates for attention. In the fifth dwelling places, our discomfort is the presence of God inviting us to inner freedom. God would have us be free for God, without attachment to even innocent things, which ultimately cannot satisfy the human heart. Learning to live in peace with our shortcomings, even to being detached from the realization of our highest ideals, is important to these dwelling places.

John of the Cross reminds us that many virtues can co-exist with imperfections, but because of the imperfections, "distraction is at least secretly caused" (A3.22.2). I understand this to mean that some distractions are subtle. These can go unnoticed if we do not have the penetrating self-knowledge that comes to us reflected in the light of God's indwelling presence. Ego contamination can sneak in unawares in spite of our desires to be completely God-oriented. Fortunately, our human limitations do not seem to be problematic for God. St. Thérèse of Lisieux understood this well. To a novice who spoke of her desire for more strength and energy with which "to practice virtue," Thérèse countered,

> And suppose God wishes to have you as feeble and powerless as a child? Do you think that would be less worthy in God's eyes? Consent to stumble, or even to fall at every step, to bear your cross feebly; love your weakness. Your soul will draw more profit from that than if, sustained by grace, you vigorously performed heroic deeds which would fill your soul with self-satisfaction and pride.[7]

---

[7] *Story of a Soul*, trans. by John Clarke, OCD (Washington, DC: ICS Publications, 1976). See pp. 239-244.

I find that as I have come to a greater acceptance of my own limitations and that of others, and as I surrender these into the heart of God's purifying love, I tend to see things in a more positive light. Since our attitudes directly affect our emotions, this more positive outlook enables me to make decisions that are more true to Jesus' gospel of love.

Rahner on Indifference

Rahner's concept of indifference is insightful and furthers our understanding of the need for the radical detachment that absolute surrender to God requires. He offers the important reminder, as do Teresa and John of the Cross, that as human beings, we are always in relation to God as our ultimate reality. Rahner's complex, but profound thought, is worth careful pondering. He writes:

> For if man [sic] is always the one who grasps the finite, individual thing in his knowledge and in his freedom in a movement directed basically toward absolute reality, toward absolute truth and goodness, in the necessary realization of his mental life he always transcends the individual thing, he dissociates himself from it, he sets the finite individual thing against a broader horizon, he rises above it, makes himself independent of it: he is "indifferent" in regard to the individual thing.[8]

Following Ignatius of Loyola, Rahner believes that indif-

---

[8] See "Indifference to All Created Things," in Karl Rahner, *The Practice of Faith: Handbook of Contemporary Spirituality* (New York: Crossroad, 1986), pp. 214-217.

ference is the essential task of our life. His reflections undergird the importance that the Carmelite tradition places on detachment. Its realization is something intrinsic to our nature. For this reason, I here digress from Teresa to Rahner. In this article on "Indifference," Rahner makes the following significant reflections. He reminds us that we grasp finite, individual things in knowledge and freedom against a broader horizon. Our human mental life in knowledge and freedom is itself that natural and supernatural basic indifference which is written in our nature. In the ground of our being is an indifference in the face of the finite, individual things, and this is disowned if we do not become indifferent, that we are in fact in process of destroying our own existence. Indifference as a task means first of all becoming open for the greater reality, which ultimately means complete openness for God. Instead, we want to grasp the individual and make it into a god, the idol of our life. We don't want to be driven out of the place where we have settled; we become mediocre; the absurd trivialities of our normal life appear to us as something great, important and significant; we cannot permit anything to be taken from us; we cannot make a sacrifice; we cannot recognize small things as small or the transitory as transitory. (This is what Teresa describes, especially of third dwelling places experiences.) Indifference opens us to the ultimate reality: God. A deep radical egoism opposes this. We keep thinking that this particular thing will make us happy. Indifference draws us into mystery. We turn from what we understand to the unfathomable depths of God.[9]

The fourth and fifth dwelling places are all about God drawing us into the depths of God, through contemplative prayer, and through touches of divine union. We do not belong to our-

---

[9]   Rahner's entire article is worth reading as it gives a theological anthropological foundation to Carmelite Spirituality.

selves, but to God. As we journey through the dwelling places, our human need for self-maintenance, self-affirmation and self-justification is transformed, encompassed and surmounted by indifference. Rahner reminds us that the process is never over. We never are truly "indifferent"; we are constantly coming to be so. This means not only daily dying with Christ, but is also the splendor of our existence. The God who is greater than we are is always revealing Godself anew in what we have surmounted, in what we have come to terms with, in what we have freely accepted.

These reflections of Rahner take us back to Teresa. Integral to indifference are simplicity and humility of heart — which Teresa deems so important, especially in these fifth dwelling places. She advises her nuns not to distract themselves by turning their attention to whether the ones to whom God grants favors are good or bad; there is no reason to meddle in the matter (V.1.8). We are to mind our own business when it comes to God, and to watch our judgmental thoughts about other persons.

God works through our and other persons' human limitations. Very holy persons can often look, and in fact be, very imperfect; this does not seem to bother God. Jesus demonstrates this by offering acceptance and peace to his disciples, in spite of their recent betrayal (see Jn 20:21).[10] Jesus' invitation: "Come to me you who are weary and troubled" (Mt 11:28-30), is an abiding enticement. What appears to be troublesome to God is when our critical eye misses what God sees is in the heart. The Pharisee could see only sin in the publican; he failed to see the publican's humble acknowledgment of his need for God (Lk 18:9-14). In these fifth dwelling places, through experiences of union with God, God begins to enlarge the heart to the capacity of Christ's accepting love.

---

[10] All three of the other evangelists have similar accounts.

To continue a now familiar theme, the subtlety of distractions along with the complexity of their meanings, as is true in other dwelling places, recurring, distracting thoughts might be inviting us to a deeper surrender. They might also be alerting us to things we should be dealing with — to our avoidance of matters that need our attention. Parents responsible for the well being of their children or persons in authority, accountable for the common good, might find in repeated distractions the voice of God calling them to responsible action when their tendency might be to let things ride. Distracting thoughts can be forceful reminders of issues we might prefer to ignore, but which need our attention. Teresa likes to remind us where true union with God is found:

> This union with God's will is the union I have desired all my life; it is the union I ask the Lord for always and the one that is safest.
> But alas for us, how few there must be who reach it; although whoever guards himself [sic] against offending the Lord and has entered religious life thinks he has done everything! Oh, but there remains some worms, unrecognized until, like those in the story of Jonah that gnawed away the ivy, they have gnawed away the virtues. This happens through self-love, self-esteem, judging one's neighbors (even though in little things), a lack of charity for them, and not loving them as ourselves. For even though, while crawling along, we fulfill our obligations and no sin is committed, we don't advance very far in what is required for complete union with the will of God (V.3.5-6).

Our feeble efforts to remain united with the will of God transform everything within the soul, even that which is dark and worm eaten. Our part, says Teresa, is to get rid of self-love, self-will and attachments (V.2.6); in other words, we are to rid ourselves of our excessive need for self-maintenance, self-affirmation and self-justification. We shift from willfulness to willingness, as Gerald May puts it.[11] Without such a shift, the depth of surrender needed for union with God cannot happen.

A Place of Creativity

The fifth dwelling places are places of creativity. The experience of union with God, even if transitory, awakens human creativity as the creative energies of God flow through the soul. Teresa describes this reality using process-images of worm, cocoon and butterfly. Her sensitivity to nature's mysteries reflects itself in an enthusiastic exposition of how the tiny silk worm becomes a beautiful butterfly in V.2.1-4. In time, the cocoon becomes too small for the developing butterfly. This holds true in the realm of the spirit. Our constricted ego-identity, characterized as self-love, self-esteem, etc., needs to expand in order to be fully transformed into the likeness of Christ. We are ready to drop the skin of our defenses and addictions, so that new behaviors and ways of being can emerge — symbolized in the butterfly. Such transformation is marvelous indeed, but it still leaves much to be done in the soul. The butterfly is fragile beauty.[12] Never-

---

[11] Gerald May in *Will and Spirit: A Contemplative Psychology* develops the process of moving from willfulness to willingness from a psychological / spiritual perspective. (San Francisco, CA: Harper & Row, 1983).

[12] In our monastery we have at times rescued monarch butterfly eggs from predators. A tiny worm emerges and feeds on milkweed. In due time the worm drops its skin and the chrysalis takes shape. One can see the tiny butterfly developing withing the chrysalis. It is an awesome moment when the chrysalis cracks open and a colorful monarch butterfly drops out and flexes its wings. It is a disheartening moment to see a butterfly (perhaps ours?) become lunch for a hungry bird. Butterflies are indeed "fragile beauty."

theless, touches of union, even thought transitory, are significant moments in the inner journey. In fact the transformation effected causes Teresa to marvel:

> ...truly I tell you that the soul doesn't recognize itself. Look at the difference there is between an ugly worm and a little white butterfly: that's what the difference is here (V.2.7).

The soul now knows by profound experiences that creatures cannot give it true rest (V.2.8), Rahner's indifference. Worldly desires come into perspective as a new consciousness takes hold. Transparency to Christ enables freedom from self-preoccupation, and from preoccupation with worldly realities that are not compatible with life in Christ. Christ instills the desire to love others as Christ loves them. Teresa says, "...a few years ago — and even perhaps days — this soul wasn't mindful of anything but itself" (V.2.10-11).

Touches of union have profound implications for societal transformation. Instinctively, the consumer, success-oriented atmosphere in which we live loses its claim as the last word in human happiness. We now know by experience that creatures cannot give us true rest (V.2.8). Worldly desires come into perspective as a new consciousness takes hold. The finality of our human life is eternal life in God. God's love stirs deep desires for God along with desires to love others as God loves them. The thoughts of the heart, which find expression in the inevitable streams of consciousness,[13] reveal less self-preoccupation and more concern for the well being of others. Why? Because God

---

[13] See Antonio Damasio, *The Feeling of What Happens: Body and Emotion in the Making of Consciousness* (San Diego, New York, London: A Harvest Book of Harcourt, Inc., 1999).

brings the soul into the inner wine cellar and puts charity in order within. The fruit of this profound experience is always good works as Teresa stresses in V.3.10-11. She offers strong advice to help us deal with our self-preoccupying thoughts should these manifest themselves. She writes:

> Let His Majesty have a free hand, for He will give you more than you know how to desire because you are striving and making every effort to do what you can about this love. And force your will to do the will of your Sisters in everything even though you may lose your rights; forget your own good for their sakes no matter how much resistance your nature puts up; and, when the occasion arises, strive to accept work yourself so as to relieve your neighbor of it. Don't think that it won't cost you anything or that you will find everything done for you. Look at what our Spouse's love for us cost Him; in order to free us from death, He died that most painful death of the cross (V.3.12).

Rightly does Teresa insist that, as followers of Christ, works are what the Lord desires. If a Sister is sick, bring her some relief and don't worry about losing devotion. If she is in pain, you feel it with her and you fast if necessary, so that she might eat.

> This is true union with His will. And if you see a person praised, the Lord wants you to be much happier than if you yourself were being praised (V.3.11).

Distractions help indicate our degree of freedom for self-giving and our ability to be for others. Does Teresa's advice about being for others in actual life-situations leave you feeling imposed upon and flooded with resentful thoughts? Such thoughts echo what is truest within. To acknowledge resentful thoughts honestly might jar our complacency, but it can also herald a path toward deeper union with God, and with our truest self. Not to acknowledge and to attend to such feelings blocks the divine energies of God from re-creating us anew so that like Teresa we too can marvel at the change we find in ourselves. We are a creation in process. God is not finished with us yet. All that Christ needs from us is a heart willing to bear the pain of growth as He transforms our weakness into strength.

> Thus, since it was He who paid the highest price, His majesty wants to join our little labors with the great ones He suffered so that all the work may become one (V.2.5).

Teresa struggles to describe the nature of the union God effects in the soul. The words of the bride in the Song of Songs, "He brought me into the wine cellar (or placed me there, I believe it says)" help Teresa to describe what it meant in her life. She continues:

> I understand this union to be the wine cellar where the Lord wishes to place us when He desires and, as He desires. But however great the effort we make to do so, we cannot enter. His majesty must place us there and enter Himself into the center of our soul (V.1.12).

Our deepest self is accessible to us only through union with God. No amount of inner work on our part does it. We can only dispose ourselves by becoming soft wax, to use Teresa's image, ready for the divine imprint (V.2.12). What a remarkable insight into the relationship between psyche and spirit. The deepest part of us — our inner depth — is accessible only through a faith-relationship with God. It is God who leads us into the deeper reaches of the human. Mysticism, one's faith-relationship with God, is integral to full human development. Unitive experiences are crucial to human life because they help shape us as loving persons. The fruit of union with God is always a deeper commitment to Christ and to Christ's gospel of love. Personal transformation is integral to societal transformation because the absence of such genuine love erodes community life, destroys marriages, weakens friendship and leads to loss of integrity in political life.

Again, when our worms resist becoming butterflies they behave like the worm that gnawed away the ivy that shaded Jonah. Jonah's ivy was superficial comfort. The worms in our lives can be even more destructive; instead of being integral to the transformation process like the little worm that becomes a butterfly, these gnaw away virtues. Teresa's words bear repetition:

> This happens through self-love, self-esteem, judging one's neighbors (even though in little things) a lack of charity for them, and not loving them as ourselves. For even though, while crawling along, we fulfill our obligation and no sin is committed, we don't advance very far in what is required for complete union with the will of God (V.3.6).

Characteristic of Teresa's continued insistence on self-knowledge, the whole of V.3 and continued in V.4 guides us in this direction. She shows ways in which the devil deceives under the color of good by darkening the intellect and cooling the will's ardor (V.4.8). *Cooling of charity*, as we have seen, is characteristic of the first dwelling places, which in its extreme, can take us to hell's frozen lake where we are up to our necks in ice because of the coldness with which we treat others.

Walter Wink, Professor of Biblical Interpretation, writes insightfully about devils and demons in scripture. He maintains that the best exorcism of all is accepting love. Fear gives the demonic its power and pulls us to worship that which enslaves us. We forge our own chains when we let our inner darkness have the last word. As Wink suggests, quoting Rainer Maria Rilke, perhaps everything terrible is in its deepest being something helpless that wants help from us.[14]

Teresa offers her own solution to fear of demons:

> First, we must always ask God in prayer to sustain us, ...we must never trust in ourselves. Then, we should walk with special care and attention, observing how we are proceeding in the practice of virtue: whether we are getting better or worse in some areas, especially in love for one another, in the desire to be considered the least among the sisters and in the performance of ordinary tasks. [She is telling us to watch out for ego inflation, which our thoughts will indicate.] For if we look out for these things and ask the Lord to enlighten us, we will soon see the gain or the loss. Don't think that a soul that comes so close to God is allowed to lose Him so quickly that the devil has an easy task. His Majesty would regret the loss of this soul so much that He gives it in many ways a thousand interior warnings, so that the harm will not be hidden from it (V.4.9).

---

14 Walter Wink, *Unmasking the Powers: The Invisible Forces That Determine Human Existence* (Philadelphia, PA: Fortress Press, 1986), p. 57.

According to Teresa, the most convincing sign of spiritual growth and the authenticity of our spiritual practice is:

> …whether we observe well the love of neighbor… for if we practice love of neighbor with great perfection, we will have done everything…. Such love must rise from love of God as its root (V.3.8-9).

The fruit of union with God is always love of neighbor, and genuine love of neighbor is always centered in union with God. Teresa concludes her discussion of the fifth dwelling places by further reflections on love of neighbor. Experiences of union with God invite holistic harmony — union with God but also harmony with one's neighbor, which ultimately means with the world community without prejudice towards race or class. Every aspect of our person reaches toward union with God. Such is the movement of the human heart. Distractions carry both information and energy toward this reality. They are the vehicles of insight into the emotions that generate persistent distracting thoughts. Emotions have no voice in themselves apart from the feelings they generate in the body. Distracting thoughts are often the voice of unacknowledged emotions. They are messengers of the inner self. The energy that shapes emotions into their own particular being, such as the energy of anger, or hurt, or jealousy, etc., becomes conscious not only through changes in the body, but also through thoughts that persist in the mind. Disturbing thoughts can be the voice of repressed or unidentified emotions awaiting conscious recognition. They want an honorable treatment; they want their voice to be heard for greater integration within our conscious life.

Anger might be asking us to protect others or ourselves in the face of real or imagined danger. Anger might be inviting us to restore something precious that has been lost. What in our lives needs to be restored? What needs to be protected? Sadness might be asking us to stop and let go of something that no longer works — a relationship, a belief or a job. Each emotion has its own message. Grief invites us to enter deeper into the river of life and truly mourn the passing of what we love and value. If we don't make that journey we are not ready for the depth of surrender that leads to an integrated life with God at the center. Grief reconnects us to life within the experience of deep and profound loss. It hollows out the soul for greater expansion as a loving person. When we step out of the river of grief we come forth cleansed of residual bitterness and resentment and therefore with an expanded capacity for love.[15] I have found that distractions torment me only when I neglect to listen to them as the word of God speaking to me through them.

Summary

A difference exists between these fifth dwelling places where experiences of mystical union with God are transitory, and the seventh dwelling places, where the soul and God are as inseparable as a drop of water in the ocean. However as we have seen, these fifth dwelling places are places of remarkable growth and creativity. Distractions in these dwelling places contain within themselves a specific invitation to self-knowledge. The disturbance and unrest they sometimes occasion, brought before Christ, can become, as it were, a hermeneutical key that can give entry to dark regions of the soul where the inflow of God is otherwise without access. As Teresa tells us, God wants everything

---

[15] I am indebted to a review of the audio tapes entitled *Emotional Genius: How Your Emotions Can Save Your Life* by Karla McLaren, found in The Sounds True Catalogue, pp. 4-5.

for God. Here, undaunted by our resistances, God draws the soul, through touches of union, toward the habitual union of the seventh dwelling places. In these fifth dwelling places, we learn by experience that the wine cellar of the soul is not accessible to us through human effort. It is God who draws us inward. To enter these deep caverns of the soul is a contemplative experience. According to Teresa, and confirmed by all the mystics of our tradition, a loving relationship with God is the key to our deepest center. A prayer-relationship with God is essential to full human development. As we experience divine unconditional love, the limits of human love begin to stretch and expand. We begin with less distracted self-preoccupation, to love others and ourselves with God's own love.

CHAPTER SIX

THE SIXTH DWELLING PLACES

...wisdom that purges and illumines the blessed spirits purges and illumines the soul here on earth
(DN 25.1).[1]

With John of the Cross's teaching about the dark night as
background, we can turn our attention to the meaning of distractions in the sixth dwelling places. These sixth dwelling places
occupy much of Teresa's attention. The first dwelling places have
two short chapters, the second only one; the third again have
two, while the fourth have three. As Teresa moves into deeper
layers of experience, the chapters increase. The fifth dwelling
places grow to four chapters while the sixth expand to eleven
chapters. The seventh dwelling places again have four comprehensive chapters, which are very important in understanding the
entire journey to the soul's center, which is God.

The dynamic of the sixth dwelling places centers on God's
invitation to prize the mystery that is us. We are God's delight.

---

[1]   For further descriptions of the dark night in John of the Cross, see: DN 2.3.3; 5.1;
6.5 also 8.3 [ray of sunlight exposes dust particles]; and 10.1 [log of wood in the
fire].

God delights in us.[2] Favors from God abound in this dwelling place, but so do trials. Life is seldom without them. However, Teresa shows how integral trials are to the process of transformation. Trials became a means of drawing Teresa beyond the limits of self into divine espousals. The interaction between trials and favors are characteristic of Teresa's transformation in these sixth dwelling places. Through her own life experience Teresa shows us how trials can lead to an increasingly focused interiority.

Many persons want a deeper entry into the house of prayer but they do not know how to engage it. For them, trials seem only a closed door instead of access into deeper realities. Through soul assimilation, trials enable a person not only "to know what one is doing when one is doing it, but also to comprehend *the meaning* of what is happening as it is happening."[3] Through more enlightened presence to one's truest self by means of presence to God, we become aware of the significance of our trials for spiritual transformation. We see the fuller meaning not only of this particular trial in the here and now instead of by hindsight, but also, through intimate Christ-awareness, our attitude toward trials in general is transformed. Therefore, in these dwelling places, while Teresa focuses on the extraordinary gifts of prayer that she receives such as visions, locutions and raptures, intermingled with these favors are descriptions of the many trials that beset her, not infrequently as a direct result of the gifts received in prayer. For Teresa, her trials open up deep dimensions of spiritual meaning so that she can now claim with certitude:

---

[2] Isaiah 62:4. For just a couple of examples in Teresa's writings, see *Spiritual Testimonies* nos. 10 and 49.

[3] See Bernard Lonergan, *Method in Theology* (London: Darton, Longman and Todd, 1971). Lonergan has much to say about the process of interiority. His levels of conversion: moral, intellectual and religious, speak to a deepened understanding of trials in human life.

This severe suffering comes that one may enter the seventh dwelling place.... These are the trials that make it (the little dove) fly still higher (VI.1.15; 2.1).[4]

Intimacy with God

The context for trials in Teresa's life is God wooing Teresa to increasingly profound experiences of intimacy (VI.2.1-2). For this reason I approach the phenomena that Teresa describes in these sixth dwelling places as the intensification, with resulting overflow into psychic and physical phenomena, of God's ever-present self-communication within the ordinary, everydayness of our lives.[5] Profound lover that God is, each moment of our lives is an abiding offer from God for loving exchange. God's self-communication may come to us in less dramatic ways, and with seeming less intensity than that experienced by Teresa; nev-

---

[4] In VI.1.1. Teresa discusses how greater trials come when the Lord begins to grant greater favors. In her *Spiritual Testimony* 58 no. 5 the process has reversed and the greater the trials, the more favors she receives.

[5] Ruth Burrows in *Interior Castle Explored* (London and Dublin: Sheed & Ward/ Veritas Publications, 1982) recognizes mystical prayer in itself as non-experiential; any accompanying phenomena is on the level of psychic experience, which Burrows disconnects from mystical prayer in its essence. While she makes some very real and helpful distinctions, I believe that the relationship between mystical graces and the phenomena Teresa experiences is far more complex than the categories "light on/light off, sensitives/non-sensitives" as Burrows presents it. This is an area that needs further study in the light of contemporary science in conversation with traditional mystical theology. *The Holographic Universe* by Michael Talbot (San Francisco: Harper/Perennial, 1991) has an interesting and informative chapter entitled "A Pocketful of Miracles." It looks at miracles and other human/ physical/spiritual phenomena from the perspective of psycho-kinesis. Other more recent material may be available that would be helpful toward such a study.

ertheless, God pursuing us is an ever-present reality.[6] While all of Teresa's writings have a way of engaging us at the deepest level of our being, this dwelling place stirs passionate longings for God, who does indeed communicate with us.

The entire *Interior Castle* is a love story, the drama of which intensifies in these sixth dwelling places. Teresa here describes in detail the ongoing narrative of God pursuing Teresa — pursuing all of us, fashioned as we are in God's image and likeness.[7] In response to God, our finite self with its limited human capacity realizes transcendence as we increasingly surrender to God's loving embrace. God the lover woos the beloved with divine favors. In the process, all that is not of God comes into sharp relief before the soul's eye. God is making room for God by illumining the clutter of things we still cling to. God entices the soul to deeper humility and freedom of spirit through painful experiences of its imperfections and sinful tendencies.

Rooms of Darkness

This is not an easy time. Although the sixth dwelling places are the places of espousal love, these are also the rooms of dark night. The brilliance of the divine presence, like the noonday sun to the unprotected eye, blinds the eyes of the soul and throws a

---

[6]   Mark McIntosh in his development of transcendentality in Rahner writes: "Because God desires communion with us we are...." In Rahner's view there never really is just human nature per se for we always bear within us the eternal echo of God's self-disclosure, and this echo within us is a fundamental structure of human being which draws us ever further into consciousness of ourselves and of the mystery which calls to us. McIntosh notes that according to Von Balthasar, we really only become the persons God created us to be insofar as we discover our true mission through participation in the mission of Christ. *Mystical Theology* (London: Blackwell Publishers, 1998), p. 93.

[7]   I.1.1. See also *Way of Perfection*, ch. 42. No. 6.

veil of darkness over God. The presence of this divine brilliance hides the face of God, even as its brightness starkly illumines all the residue of sin in the soul. Teresa elaborates in detail the many ways in which God purifies the soul. The descriptions of her own dark times are important in that they point to the reality that purification happens, not in abstraction, but right within the everydayness of each person's life. What she describes is particular to her unique experience, but it easily translates into contemporary situations and inter-personal relationships. The harsh judgments, criticism and misunderstandings Teresa experiences are not unique to her. Nor are some of her understandable reactions as in VI.1.13, where she describes her struggles in prayer and how these affect her emotionally, as we shall see further on.

Interplay between Favors and Trials

Teresa seems intent on helping us realize that trials have an important role to play in our life of prayer; that embracing darkness is a critical and significant movement in the journey toward divine union. The interplay between favors and trials make the sixth dwelling places, par excellence, rooms of paradox. The diamond castle of the soul here undergoes the polishing of God's intimate presence in Christ. Love's purifying fire ignites everything within or around us that attempts to exist outside of the divine ambiance; whatever resists the inflow of God in the depth of our spirit is being purified and transformed. God, who woos us, is the same God who purifies us for God. The inner eye is being enlightened, and the soul educated to the profound understanding that darkness in prayer, physical pain, difficult life situations and the torments of temptation, are mysteriously pregnant with the energies of the Risen Christ. As Teresa repeatedly attests, favors and trials follow each other. The tension between the abiding "favor" of God's indwelling presence interacting with our human fragility, and tendency to sin, resolves itself only in surrender of the self to God in trust and abandonment.[8] More difficult still is believing that the "experience" of no experience at all — not even dryness — *just nothing*, can have meaning in our life with God.

Faith: The Language of the Soul

The "experience" of no experience calls for an ever deeper faith as our psyche, our outer and inner sensing capacities, along with our deeper spirit, become sensitized to the impact *of God making room for God* which is the work of God in these dwelling places.[9] This process calls forth a unique faith response on our part so that we become increasingly fluent in the language of human/divine communication. *Faith* is the language of the spirit in communion with God. It is knowledge of God born of love.[10] Faith, hope and love exist in dynamic communion as a single, interactive reality.

---

[8] For an interesting contemporary hermeneutic of abandonment and surrender see *Powers and Submissions: Spirituality, Philosophy, and Gender* by Sarah Coakley (London: Blackwell Publishers, 2002). Chapter One entitled "Kenosis and Subversion: On the Repression of 'Vulnerability' in Christian Feminist Writings" is of particular note.

[9] Iain Matthew in *The Impact of God*, in a very readable fashion, shows how God makes room for God through the life and teachings of John of the Cross (London: Hodder & Stoughton, 1995).

[10] See Lonergan, *Method in Theology*, pp. 112-118.

The Dynamic of Faith, Hope and Love

Believing, hoping and loving are at the heart of all relationships both human and divine. But a vast difference exists. Human relatedness happens initially, through a process of physical presence. We see each other with our eyes, and we hear each other with our ears, assuming we are not visually or hearing impaired. With God it is different. We cannot see God the way we see one other; nor can we hear God in the same manner that we can hear one other. At the same time — and this is integral to the paradox of this dwelling place — we do, in a sense, see God with the inner eye of love, and we do hear God speak through the ears of the heart as God communicates with us. However, as John of the Cross points out, "The clearer and the more obvious divine things are in themselves, the darker and the more hidden they are to the soul naturally" (DN 2.5.3). God would transform our human mode of communicating with a transcendent quality — with what are called the supernatural virtues of faith, hope and love. Virtue derives from the Latin, *virtus*, which means strength. Faith, hope and love are to prayer somewhat like the foundations of a building that give it strength and endurance. These virtues are the foundational language of prayer, and are the means toward union with God. Regardless of the manner in which we pray, unless our prayer is grounded in faith, hope and love, our prayer lacks energy for spiritual transformation. Once the soul is united with God, "it is always so closely joined to His Majesty that from this union comes its fortitude" (VI.1.2).

Methods of Prayer/Importance of Never Abandoning Christ

Prayer can take many forms. Vocal prayer gives verbal expression to our communion with God. When this takes place interiorly, as silent words directed to God, or to the saints, or when we reflect on the mysteries of Christ, we practice what Teresa calls mental prayer. At times, utter silence is the only adequate response to the experience of divine, self-giving love. The language of prayer then becomes the silence of mystical speech. Words become increasingly inadequate the more divine love draws the soul into intimate communion. Such depth of intimacy with God not only silences speech, but also absorbs into itself the flow of thought that otherwise invades conscious life. Distracting thoughts are awed to rest. In VI.7.5-15 Teresa offers insights especially helpful for such transitional times of moving toward deeper silence in our prayer journey. Here she reiterates the importance of the humanity of Christ to our prayer. Contemplative silence, and absorption in God, needs the support of Christ and his gospel message to keep the soul grounded in reality. "To be always withdrawn from corporeal things and enkindled in love is the trait of angelic spirits not of those who live in mortal bodies" (VI.7.6). Teresa reasons that this is so because:

> ...in meditation the whole effort is in seeking God and that once God is found the soul becomes used to seeking Him again through the work of the will, the soul doesn't want to tire itself by working with the intellect. Likewise, it seems to me that since this generous faculty, which is the will is already enkindled, it wants to avoid, if it can, using the other faculty; and it doesn't go wrong. But to avoid this will be impossible, especially before the soul reaches these last two dwelling places; and the soul will lose time, for the will often needs the help of the intellect so as to be enkindled (VI.7.7).

Distractions

Our reflections thus far are important to what follows. They serve as helps toward understanding Teresa's insights in these sixth dwelling places in regard to our struggle with distractions. While the word, "distraction," does not appear in these sixth dwelling places, there are however, references to the "wandering of the mind" within the context of a kind of mindless absorption, that Teresa considers a waste of time. As she describes it:

> ...the mind wandered here and there. My soul, it seems to me, was like a bird flying about that doesn't know where to light; and it was losing a lot of time and not making progress in virtue or improving in prayer (VI.7.15).

Two things of particular note are: first, that mindless absorption, which differs from focused centering prayer, or the forms of quiet prayer Teresa describes, distracts us from truly praying and from mindfulness of Christ in our prayer, and second, it leaves the mind open for endless wandering.

> Moreover, daughters, enjoyment in prayer is not so habitual that there is not time for everything. I would be suspicious of anyone who says this delight is continual (VI.7.13).
>
> The mistake it seemed to me that I was making wasn't so extreme, rather it consisted of not delighting so much in the thought of our Lord Jesus Christ but in going along in that absorption, waiting for that enjoyment. And I realized clearly that I was proceeding badly. Since it wasn't possible for me to experience

the absorption always, the mind wandered here and there. My soul, it seems to me, was like a bird flying about that doesn't know where to light; and it was losing a lot of time and not making progress in virtue or improving in prayer (VI.7.15).

The attempt to simulate God's gift in prayer, which Teresa calls "mindless absorption," creates the perfect set-up for the mind to wander. Not only do we expose ourselves to the wanderings of the mind, but also, as Teresa insists, we lose a lot of time, and we stagnate both in prayer and in life. An important message in my own early formative days in Carmel was: "Pray as you can and not as you can't."[11] If a person is not able to meditate, Teresa offers the alternative of simple presence to Christ without discursive thought: someone must necessarily blow on the fire so that heat will be given off (VI.7.8). We are not to be like dunces wasting time waiting for what was given us once before (VI.7.9). The mysteries of Christ are always available as ever-present nourishment, if not through reflective meditation, at least by way of a simple gaze or quiet mindfulness that sparks love (VI.7.11).

Advice about Prayer

Consistently does Teresa ground prayer in the reality of human inadequacy before God. This is a recurring theme throughout Teresa's writings, which she here emphasizes in chapter seven of these dwelling places. The deepest desires of the heart

---

[11] I subsequently learned that it is Dom John Chapman who offers this timeless advice in his *Spiritual Letters* (London, 1935), p. 109: "Pray as you can and do not try to pray as you can't."

are for God, yet divine communication, which God's intimate presence to human life calls forth from us, is necessarily channeled through our humanity, that is, through human finitude. This means that without the purification that exercises faith and deepens love, human nature of itself cannot take too much of God. Our inner self too easily gets cluttered with that which obscures God's self-communication. Even desire for God can be contaminated with the residue of sinful desires, as Teresa is profoundly aware:

> These favors are like waves of a large river in that they come and go; but the memory these souls have of their sins clings like thick mire. It seems that these sins are alive in the memory, and this is a heavy cross (VI.7.2).

According to John of the Cross, even though the soul is at an advanced stage of the spiritual journey, the stains of the old self still linger in the spirit. Our subtle attachments are many, and so even the desire for God can have its own prideful delusions. John of the Cross exposes these hidden realities with clarity and directness when he writes:

> These proficients also have the *hebetudo mentis*, the natural dullness everyone contracts through sin, and a distracted and inattentive spirit. The spirit must be illumined, clarified, and recollected by means of the hardships and conflicts of this night (DN 2.2.1-2).[12]

John draws our attention to more subtle layers of distrac-

---

[12] As Kavanaugh points out, an important factor in John's anthropology is that sin lies at the root of all the defects mentioned in Book One and Book Two of the *Dark Night*, p. 397.

tion. That we be aware of them is important if we are to journey deeper in our love-relationship with God.

Not only the mind, but the *spirit* also can be *inattentive and
distracted* from its transcendent orientation toward union with
God. The remains of sin still cling to this deep place within the
self. John deals with issues of presumption, pride, vanity and arrogance (DN 2.2.3). Vices such as these blur the eyes of the spirit
causing us to live out of a myopic vision of what it means to be
fully human. Surrender of the self to God ultimately frees the
self from the clinging myth of self-fulfillment, from taints of ego
inflation and self-centeredness. At the same time, subtle forms
of "vanity," as well as "arrogance" paradoxically, can mask feelings of self-doubt, worthlessness and ineptitude for both women
and men. Ego inflation, expressed as either vanity or arrogance,
along with feelings of worthlessness, can be manifestations of
residual pride lingering deep in the spirit.[13] Rather than humbly
acknowledging to ourselves the human reality of sin, finitude,
limit, and incompleteness, we cover our innate insecurity with
a veneer of superiority, or spiritual excellence. Genuine inner
security is found in God, not in creatures, and least of all, not
within the self apart from God. When we are secure in God,
human limitations, even our sinful tendencies, instead of causing disturbance, become a source of humility, and offer occasion for conversion and transformation. We no longer have need

---

[13] Valerie Savings offers the reality that temptations of women as women are not
the same as temptations of men as men. Pride expresses itself in men more likely
as will to power, control and domination. The sins of women are more likely to be
associated with "frivolity, distractability, and diffuseness; lack of an organizing
center or focus; dependence on others for one's own self-definition; tolerance at
the expense of standards of excellence; inability to respect the boundaries of pri-
vacy; sentimentality; gossipy sociability, and mistrust of reason; in short, under-
development or negation of the self." Valerie Savings, "The Human Situation: A
Feminine View" reprinted in Carol P. Christ and Judith Plaskow (eds.) *Womanspirit
Rising: A Feminist Reader in Religion* (San Francisco, CA: HarperSF, 1992 reprint
paperback edition), p. 37.

to "put on this outward show," as Teresa is accused of doing (VI.1.3). Faults and failings do not disturb a heart whose strength issues from communion with God as abiding presence.

When we are open to God in prayer, the light of Christ's indwelling Spirit shining within, reveals the prideful expressions of our otherwise unrecognized, *distracted and inattentive spirit.* Exposed in God's light, these unwelcome dimensions of the self, invite us to acknowledge their existence and to surrender all that is not of God into God's awaiting heart. The God of these sixth dwelling places mirrors us to ourselves. In God, the lines of the "inner sketch," which is both that of God, and the soul, come to completion through Christ's purifying, transforming love. Fulfillment of the self in God, the completion of the sketch through faith-filled surrender, is the work of the dark night.[14]

> This dark night is an inflow of God into the soul, which purges it of its habitual ignorance and imperfections, natural and spiritual, and which the contemplatives call infused contemplation or mystical theology.... Insofar as infused contemplation is loving wisdom of God, it produces two principal effects in the soul: by purging and illumining, this contemplation prepares the soul for union with God through love. Hence the same loving wisdom that purges and illumines the blessed spirits purges and illumines the soul here on earth (DN 2.5.1).

---

[14] *Spiritual Canticle*, stanza 12: "O spring like crystal! If only, on your silvered-over faces, you would suddenly form the eyes I have desired, which I bear sketched deep within my heart." In stanza 11.12 and stanza 12.1, "the sketch" is simultaneously the bride and the Bridegroom. Chapter Two, "Entering the Empty Spaces of the Encounter" in *The Footprints of Love: John of the Cross as Guide in the Wilderness* by Hein Blommestijn, Jos Huls, Kees Waaijman (Leuven: Peeters, 2000), translated by John Vriend, offers an insightful understanding of the relationship between the experience of the self and the experience of God.

The truth of God's transcendence ultimately shines through the soul, as increasingly it becomes God by participation. As the self is purified, false and inadequate notions both of the self *and* of God inevitably come into sharp relief.

These proficients are still very lowly and natural in their communion with God and in their activity directed toward Him because the gold of the spirit is not purified and illumined. They still think of God and speak of Him as little children, and their knowledge and experience of Him is like that of little children, as St. Paul asserts (1 Cor 13:11; DN 2.3.3).

For Teresa, one of the benefits of the favors she receives is a more profound awareness of, and reverence for, this God who communicates so lovingly with her. "It is astonished at how bold it was; it weeps over its lack of respect" (VI.7.2). Her greatest affliction seems to be an ever deepened sense of how ungrateful she has been toward the One to whom she owes so much. "For in these grandeurs God communicates to it, it understands much more about Him" (VI.7.2).

The inflow of God as "loving wisdom" purifies and transforms our immature, too small, human, projected images of God. As God's loving wisdom diffuses itself through the soul, what is less than God, no longer finds space to exist, and so it disappears into dark oblivion, leaving behind a void, and seeming absence of God. Letting go of a recognizable god of our own making for the God of incomprehensible mystery who now claims the rooms of the heart, is integral to our journey through these sixth dwelling places.[15]

Understanding our dark times is important to the dynamic of distractions in the sixth dwelling places. Teresa makes many

---

[15] See DN 2.5.1. Women and men today tell of experiences of God beyond traditional, patriarchal God-images. Such a shift can be painful as well as liberating, as immature images of both God and the self are purified and transformed.

allusions to "the wandering of the mind" (distractions), in reference to discerning when favors are authentic or not. Her astute reflections for discerning the authenticity of locutions and other "favors," proves to be sound advice for dealing with distractions. In the earlier dwelling places, distractions can expose attachments that have root causes in various forms of narcissistic injury; in childhood developmental patterns, which tended to stunt emotional growth; in psychological issues involving childhood trauma, etc., or simply from the emotional residue of difficult experiences inevitable to even normal childhood development. However, as we have been considering, what is at issue in these sixth dwelling places, is something deeper. God is making room for God through the purification of the dark night, which lays bare "our distracted and inattentive spirit." This process takes us into more profound regions of the self where "experience of God and experience of self are one."[16] The roots of sin within the *spirit*, unreachable to human effort, within the dynamic of the dark night, are purified and transformed by love.

Sorrow for sin and its avoidance leave intact the roots of our sinful inclinations, even though we may have put to rest sin's external manifestations. In these sixth dwelling places, Teresa writes about the dark night as she herself experienced it, precipitated by the interaction between favors and trials. The sufferings occasioned by her mystical graces exposed, and purified, the root causes of her distractions, her "inattentive spirit."

---

[16] See Karl Rahner, "Experience of Self and Experience of God" in *Theological Investigations*, Vol. 13 (New York: Crossroad, 1983).

Teresa's Inattentive Spirit

The fifth dwelling places leave the soul filled with great desires for God and "fully determined to take no other spouse"
(VI.1.1). And yet so great a favor is not without cost. Teresa's
realism reminds us: "I doubt very much that those persons who
sometimes enjoy so truly the things of heaven will live free of
earthly trials that come in one way or another." She would have
us be rid of everything that could be an obstacle to this solitude
— which is our union with God (VI.1.1). Life's "everydayness"
brings trials sufficient for our transformation, as they did for Teresa, if we allow God to purify us through them. Teresa vividly
describes the cumulative burden of trials confronting her at this
time in her spiritual journey. In spite of God's profound self-
communication to Teresa through mystical graces, she feels everything is lost. People gossip about her, friends turn away, and
they express disbelief of her gifts: "She has gone astray." Confessors doubt her (VI.1.3). In the face of Teresa's sense of un-
worthiness before God, praise itself becomes an intolerable burden (VI.1.4). Physical illness regularly afflicts her (VI.1.6). Critics
judge her gifts in prayer, with its accompanying favors, to be from
the devil or from melancholy, which leaves her soul tormented
and disturbed. In times of dryness, past favors appear to be an
illusion, and so it seems to the soul that it has never been mindful of God and never will be; God seems far away (VI.1.8). The
soul's understanding is so darkened that it cannot explain itself;
it becomes incapable of seeing the truth and believes whatever
the imagination represents to it. It is made to think that God
rejects it. It suffers unbearable interior oppression like that of
hell.[17] Reading is without comprehension, for the intellect is in-

---

[17] See *The Book of Her Life*, Chapter 32, where she describes a vision in which she
sees her place in hell.

capable of understanding (VI.1.9). The soul feels no consolation in prayer: "If it prays, it feels as though it hasn't prayed — as far as consolation goes. Solitude causes greater harm — and also another torment for this soul is that it be with anyone, or that others speak to it" (VI.1.13).

Much as she tries, in spite of her feelings of ingratitude, Teresa cannot hide the favors God lavishes upon her. These elicit unkind words and uncharitable gossip:

> She's trying to make out she's a saint; she goes to extremes to deceive the world and bring others to ruin; there are better Christians who do not put on all this outward show.[18]

Referring to herself, Teresa continues:

> Those she considered her friends turn away from her, and they are the ones who take the largest and most painful bite at her: "That soul has gone astray and is clearly mistaken; these were things of the devil; she will turn out like this person or that other that went astray, and will bring about a decline in virtue; she has deceived her confessors" (and they go to these confessors, telling them so, giving examples of what happened to some that were lost in this way); a thousand kinds of ridicule and statements like the above (VI.1.3).

We are not left to imagine the distracting thoughts such gossip generates in Teresa. The text speaks for itself. With self-

---

[18] In the fifth dwelling places she wisely comments: "Great are the wiles of the devil; to make us think we have one virtue — when we don't — he would circle hell a thousand times." V.3.9.

defensive vigor, Teresa comments in parenthesis, "And it's worth noting that she is not putting on any outward show but just striving to fulfill well her state in life" (VI.1.3). How much we suffer when people misjudge our behavior, or when we are wrongly accused. The late Cardinal Bernardin was falsely accused of sexual misconduct. Under such circumstances, we can empathize with the feelings and thoughts that might plague the mind, and stir up residue of unpurified sinful inclinations. We know that these did not have the last word for Cardinal Bernardin. His heart found forgiveness for his perpetrator. The experience, no doubt, was integral to his spiritual transformation.[19]

Through vivid accounts of her own trials in this dwelling place, and how she deals with them, Teresa help us to see how difficult life situations, severe illness, misunderstanding and blame, can become good compost for God's transforming action.[20] Our trials in life may be less dramatic than those of Teresa, but at one time or another, inevitably do difficult situations confront us, perhaps with great severity. These have a way of challenging deeply entrenched manners of being, thinking and relating. Even our best efforts at being true to Christ and his gospel of love, now find us wanting. Instinctive unloving attitudes of spirit surface to roam the mind, and to expose how contaminated love is. Even the slightest remains of narcissistic enmeshment, of inflated ego, or of prideful attachments, which clutter space in the heart that belongs to God, now stare us in

---

[19] I have a physician friend who looked forward to his retirement in order to take time "to smell the roses," as he put it, who recently said to me after a reflective morning working in his garden, "You know, as a doctor I listened to many people tell me about the struggles and sufferings that came their way. I think purgatory is in this life, and not something that is meant to happen to us after we die." John of the Cross compares the purification of the dark night to purgatory, e.g., in A1.4.3; DN 2.6.6; 10.5; 20.5; LF 1.21.24.

[20] See "Crisis and Transformation: Turning Over the Compost" in *The Way* (London: Heythrop College), January 2004.

the face. We suffer at the sight of our own unloveliness. Spiritual marriage seems an impossible dream and passion for God runs cold. As Teresa describes it: the soul's understanding is darkened, and it becomes incapable of seeing the truth (VI.1.9); the devil makes it think that it is rejected by God (VI.1.9); pains in the body afflict the soul (VI.1.6); grace is hidden, it feels it has no love of God (VI.1.11). The soul can do nothing but wait for the mercy of God (VI.1.10).

The Purpose of Teresa's and Our Suffering: Centering the Soul in God

What is the purpose of it all? "God want us to know our own misery and that God is king; and this is very important for what lies ahead" (VI.1.12). As we have seen, "This severe suffering comes so that one may enter the seventh dwelling place" (VI.1.15). The work of God in the sixth dwelling places is to center the soul totally in God. Through difficult life experiences, God alerts us to everything about ourselves that still resists being for God. Teresa has walked the journey and she encourages us not to cover over our less seemly reactions, nor the inevitable dark, recurring thoughts that circle the mind in the face of unjust blame, misunderstandings, sudden discovery of serious illness and the like. God does not inflict these human realities, but God does use them for our ultimate good. Trials of this nature invite us to surrender in prayer these hidden forces in the human soul which give rise to disordered energy, and to an inattentive, distracted spirit. They expose deep layers of illusion and self-deception that easily contaminate even our best intent. Along with the pain of darkness is the pain of light, exposing what we might prefer to leave hidden. As God increasingly makes room for God, the divine presence starkly illumines the many ways in which our demons assert themselves with sly words of self-conceit, and with visions of hope that are sheer illusion. Much that enraptures us is now recognized as empty of ultimate satisfaction. Everything within and around us that does not foster a deeper relationship with God, now stares us in the face, often to our dismay.

Teresa's self-description, during a time of severe trial, hardly fits our image of what saints should be like. At a time when she has no consolation in prayer, when physical sufferings are intense and exacerbated by other afflictions, speaking in the third person, she writes:

> If it prays, it feels as though it hasn't prayed — as far as consolation goes ... solitude causes greater harm — and also another torment for this soul is that it be with anyone or that others speak to it.... And thus however much it forces itself not to do so, it goes about with a gloomy and ill-tempered mien that is externally very noticeable (VI.1.13).

In times of darkness, dryness or just plain indifference, in the experience of no experience, to have the memory search out Jesus, who knew many trials and dark hours in his short life and tragic death, becomes Teresa's remedy for her inattentive and distracted spirit as God increasingly prepares Teresa for the fullness of divine union.[21] We have already seen the significance that Teresa places on the humanity of Christ. For a brief period of time she actually abandoned her "guide, the good Jesus" in a mistaken belief that the humanity of Christ is a hindrance to

---

[21] See *Way of Perfection*, Chapter 26, where Teresa describes a method for recollecting one's mind through attentiveness to Christ.

contemplative prayer (VI.7.15).[22] She recognizes that the inflow of God often leaves a person unable to use the intellect or engage in discursive thought as a form of meditation. However, through personal experience, Teresa is acutely aware that always to be completely occupied in love is not possible. We need to "blow on the fire so that heat will be given off." This is particularly true in seasons of dryness. Here it is that Teresa strongly advises that we not "lose the guide, who is the good Jesus." So emphatic is Teresa that she describes the difference between meditation, "I means discursive reflection with the intellect," and a simple representation in the intellect and holding in memory Christ in one of his mysteries. Especially significant for times of dryness when God's presence is not felt, should "such a person walk continually in an admirable way with Christ, our Lord, in whom the divine and the human are joined and who is always that person's companion."[23] Regularly does Teresa refer to the "*mysteries* of the most sacred humanity of our Lord Jesus Christ." These events are more than historical realities — they are *mysteries* to be contemplated, to be held in loving remembrance. The events in the life of the historical Jesus are *mysteries* because for Teresa the historical Jesus and the Risen Christ are inseparable.

John of the Cross severely admonishes spiritual directors who impose meditation on persons in whom God is secretly and quietly infusing loving knowledge in the soul. He encourages persons to remain in simple loving awareness of God and he gives clear signs as to when a person is to let go of more active meditation and allow themselves to be receptive before the inflow of God.[24] In chapter nine of *The Book of Her Life*, Teresa describes

---

[22] In Chapter 22 of *The Book of Her Life* she develops at length the significance of the humanity of Christ to contemplative prayer.

[23] VI.7.9.

[24] In LF 3.33; A2.13; DN 1.9.2-4, John of the Cross gives us signs for discerning when the soul is being drawn from meditation to contemplation.

her method of keeping Christ present, since she herself could not reflect discursively with the intellect. In these sixth dwelling places (VI.7.7) she also offers advice for persons for whom discursive thought in prayer is difficult.

Signs for Sorting Distractions

Along with advice for keeping the soul focused on Christ, in these sixth dwelling places, Teresa also gives us signs for discerning the truth and the falseness of the heart's dynamics and the thoughts that these generate. Her dark night often focuses on the struggle to understand when favors are from God, and when they are from the devil, or sources other than God, since these favors are what cause foes, and sometimes friends, to criticize her and label her as deluded. The professional theologians, as well as her confessors, are of no help. On the contrary, they often add to her pain because they lack understanding of mystical graces. Teresa agonizes over ways to authenticate her experiences, confronted as she is with doubt and condemnation from the learned men whom she consults. She is forced to look within for signs to indicate when the visions, raptures and locutions that she experiences, are from God, and when they are from the devil, or mere delusion. At a glance, in these sixth dwelling places, I counted over ten such attempts on the part of Teresa to sort out her experiences.[25] Chapters two and three in particular give repeated examples of this process from which we can benefit.

---

[25] Major texts in *The Interior Castle* where Teresa deals with signs of discernment regarding religious experience include: VI.2.6; VI.3.5; 10, 17; VI.4.11; VI.5.10, 12; VI.6.3; VI.7.8-9, 15.

Locutions

Teresa deals at length with validating locutions. To help herself, she begins by reflecting on the experience: locutions are specific inner words with a divine message, and are a very different experience from random, distracting thoughts. According to Teresa, locutions are communicated in various ways:

> Some seem to come from outside oneself; others, from deep within the interior part of the soul; still others, from the superior part; and some are so exterior that they come through the sense of hearing for it seems there is a spoken word (VI.3.1).

From her experience, she observes that locutions offer direction, insight, or meaning for life.

I will spend some time with Teresa's signs of discernment because I believe they are helpful in understanding the meaning of, and dealing with, distractions in these sixth dwelling places. According to Teresa, when locutions are from God, certain signs are present.

> **First and truest** is the power and authority they bear. (They effect what they say — "It is I fear not" and fear is taken away).
> **The second sign** is the great quiet left in the soul, the devout and peaceful recollection and readiness to engage in the praises of God.
> **The third sign** is that the words remain in the memory a long time (VI.3.5-7; see also VI.3.11).

When locutions come from the imagination, none of these signs is evident: neither certitude, nor peace, nor interior delight

(VI.3.10). According to Teresa, persons of weak constitution can think that words heard while in a dream-like state are the voice of God, or if with affection they are begging our Lord for something, they think the locution is telling them what they want to hear. God does speak to us through our dreams, but here Teresa means a kind of a dreamy state of consciousness in which the imagination takes over (VI.3.10).

Our imagination can indeed deceive us, but more seriously, deceptions can also come from the devil. Devils loom large in Teresa's 16th century world-view.[26] The devil can counterfeit locutions and can say words very clearly so that there will be certitude about their meaning. What the devil cannot do however, is to produce the effects of God's visitation, which are peace or light in the soul; on the contrary, the devil leaves restlessness and disturbance. For our encouragement, Teresa assures us that the devil can do little harm, or none at all, if the soul is humble. She adds further clarification:

1. One thing very certain is that when the spirit is from God the soul esteems itself less the greater the favor granted.
2. It has more awareness of its sins and is forgetful of its own gain.
3. Its will and memory are employed more in seeking only the honor of God, nor does it think of its own profit.
4. It walks with greater fear lest its will deviate in anything and with greater certitude that it never deserved any of those favors but deserved hell (VI.3.17).

---

[26] I suggest that the demonic is anything that robs us of our freedom to choose the good. We daily encounter demons of consumerism, demons that engender a false sense of entitlement, demons of political and economic corruption, demons that exploit the environment for human greed, etc.

Teresa also insists that words spoken by God have certain persistence; the soul is forced to listen because in the process, God puts a stop to all other thoughts, and makes the soul attend to what is said. It would be more possible for a person with very good hearing not to hear someone else speaking in a loud voice, for such a person could turn attention away and center the mind and intellect on something else. But in the locution from God, there are no ears to stop, nor is there the power to think of anything but what is said to the soul. All of this brings deep humility and the realization that another greater Lord than itself governs that castle (VI.3.17-18).

Teresa's Three Signs of Discernment Applied to Distractions

Distractions are different from locutions in that a genuine locution is the divine presence heard within the soul with a specific message or intent, while distractions are our own emotions, psyche or spirit making themselves heard. In spite of this difference, I believe that from Teresa's experience with locutions, and her reflections on the phenomenon, we can find help in dealing with those pesky things we call distractions. First we will consider what Teresa's insights might mean for distractions — regardless of their source — and then see how they serve as a guide in identifying distractions that are particular to the sixth dwelling places.

I begin with some general considerations. In discerning when locutions are from God, Teresa says they contain an inner power and authority. They effect what they say. Applying this to distractions, since nothing is outside of God's loving and creating presence, we can believe for our encouragement, that even disturbing or just plain persistent thoughts contain within themselves constructive energy for personal growth. Underneath the thoughts that distract us are emotions that find a voice in these thoughts. If we ignore disturbing distractions or try to brush them away, the emotion remains within like a volcano preparing to erupt. But if we take time to be present to the distraction by looking underneath it in search of the emotion that generates the distraction, we tap into energy to do something about what is troubling and calling for our attention. If we bring our faith in God's abiding presence to the disturbing experience, we can say with Teresa that our persistent distracting words are of God (locutions that come from God have a persistence) and we can trust that God will guide us to appropriate action.

For example: if something disturbing happens in community, instead of letting it replay itself in my mind throughout the rest of the day, and letting my feelings about it intensify, I take a quiet moment of attentiveness to God, attentiveness to my distracting thoughts, and especially to the feelings these thoughts generate. In a particular situation, I identified a feeling of anger. Like all created reality, anger is a creature of God, so first I embraced it and then I placed myself, and the feelings of anger, in God's hands. Instead of denying or ignoring the anger, I embraced it before God and in doing so I felt a shift within. The anger turned into energy for constructive action. Instead of going distractedly around and around what was annoying me, my thoughts and my feelings, now centered in God, suggested something positive that I could do to ease the situation. The problem was still there, but I felt less helpless in the face of it. I would do what was possible, and leave the rest in God's hands, where it belonged (as a wise spiritual guide often reminded me). Through this prayerful process, I had turned my disturbing, distracting thoughts into effective action, and I benefitted by a fuller surrender of my life to God.

Teresa's second sign of discernment is a great quiet left in the soul, a devout and peaceful recollection, and the readiness to engage in the praises of God. In the instance described above, I returned to my work with a quiet, recollected heart. Distractions regarding the situation no longer plagued me once I did what was in my power to do, and I felt an inner freedom as I placed the rest in God's hands.

What about the third sign: that the words remain in memory for a very long time? After experiences like the one just mentioned, what I find remains in memory is the inner certitude that God is in charge, and that I need to remain in an attitude of surrender to the presence and activity of God in this, as in all life situations. God is always, everywhere intimately present to, and within the human story. This kind of certitude implants itself in the heart when we allow faith to illumine our distractions. Different from idle passivity, surrender to God leaves the heart and mind free to consider constructive action on our part. When we listen to our distractions without taking time to honestly connect to the feelings that energize them, and without recourse to God's indwelling Spirit, we may impulsively determine a course of action that is but the projection outward of unnamed feelings. Unacknowledged anger, resentment and the like, can precipitate action that becomes destructive to all persons involved. When we are out of touch with our feelings, the mind tends to rationalize and to tell us what we want to hear, as Teresa says of locutions not from God.

What happens when we do not let our faith in God's abiding presence help us in dealing with distraction? I suspect that we run into all the things that Teresa attributes to the devil. We have no certitude regarding appropriate action; we have neither peace nor interior delight. On the contrary instead of peace and light in the soul, we are left with restlessness and disturbance. When we deliberately entertain dark, discouraging thoughts, or thoughts of self-pity, these inevitably draw us into our inner "black hole" where resentment, uncontrolled anger, and all that is destructive and oppressive between persons, has its origin. In difficult life situations, the "devil" tempts us to see only the dark side, so we lose perspective. We become vulnerable to hopelessness, depression and an unforgiving heart.

Teresa wisely insists that if locutions concern something serious about oneself that has to be carried out in deed, or business affairs involving third parties, nothing should ever be done or pass through one's mind without the opinion of a learned and prudent confessor and servant of God (VI.3.10-11). When distractions leave us disturbed and agitated, in such a case, before we take any action, Teresa would have us seek wise counsel. Check it out with someone who can be objective, and who can help you get in touch with deeper, unacknowledged issues around whatever is being obsessive in thought. Persistent dreams can be a word from God inviting attention, or they can reflect some dark part of us needing the exorcism of faith and surrender to God.

Here again Teresa leaves us with signs of discernment as to how well we are dealing with the conversion of spirit that distractions here call forth (VI.3.17). She says the soul esteems itself less and has more awareness of its own sins. Bringing faith to bear on our distractions should result in less ego-inflation. We come to a more realistic self-image and are ready to come off of the cloud of idealism. We can let go of our self-righteousness and our judgmental attitude that often reflects more about ourselves than about the actual situation. In befriending our own and others' imperfections, we, as it were, "join the human race" — we can acknowledge ourselves, in true humility, as members of the "communion of sinners" with the rest of humankind. Thoughts born of an inflated ego invite conversion of heart, so that we become less judgmental of others, less self-centered, and better able to see others through the eyes of God. Teresa says that our will and memory are employed more in seeking only the honor of God, nor do we think about our own profit (VI.3.17). We come to appropriate self-diffidence. In a word, we learn to be humble in the truth of ourselves as fragile, finite even sinful, yet as infinitely loved by God.

Applications Specific to the Sixth Dwelling Places

Whenever we are at the threshold of going deeper in our life with God, which is what the sixth dwelling places are specifically about, we are especially vulnerable to temptations of the devil. According to the dictionary definition, the word "distraction" comes from the Latin, "distractus" or "distrahere." It gives these sets of meaning:

1. To pull in different directions and separate.

2. To turn or draw from an object; to divert from any point or toward various other objects. To draw toward different, conflicting objects; to fill with different considerations, to perplex, to confound; to harass, to be troubled in mind.

3. To disorder the reason; to derange the regular operations of the intellect; to render insane; to craze.

In the sixth dwelling places, distractions, like inner persistent words, can perplex, confound, harass and trouble the mind, and feel diabolic in nature. Persistent dark thoughts, not grounded in a specific personal reality, can torment us. We seem to have no avenue of escape from their persistence. We are strongly tempted to follow their destructive urgings, and can resist only by frequent cries to God for help. But even God seems uninterested in our plight. If the experience is truly a dark night temptation, neither therapy nor spiritual direction will be able to offer insight or relief. All we can do is: "Let the pain of it get to you since God isn't finished with you yet" — again from a wise spiritual guide during one of my own darkest hours. "There is no remedy for this tempest," writes Teresa, "but to wait for the mercy of God" (VI.1.10). When temptation's work is done, and we are released from what feels like an eternity of hell, we will find ourselves freer for God with a new vision of reality before us.[27] Everything in life is now seen as energized with the power of Christ's risen life. All that is of earth is seen to be also of God.

In VI.5.10 Teresa again gives signs as to the effects of God's work in the soul that are valuable tools for measuring spiritual growth such as:

> Knowledge of the grandeur of God;
>
> Self-knowledge and humility upon seeing that something so low in comparison with the Creator of so many grandeurs dared to offend Him;
>
> Little esteem of earthly things save for those that can be used for the service of so great a God. These are the jewels the Spouse begins to give the betrothed...

We began by saying that Teresa's experience was uniquely hers. She lived in 16th century Spain. Her perception of the universe was limited to the science of her day and the myths surrounding it. At the same time, her mystical vision did indeed give her a profound perception of the grandeur of God as

---

[27] Apropos of our own dark times, Rahner has a wonderful commentary on Jesus' descent into darkness. He writes: "Christ descended into the heart of all that tempts us.... Christ ascended into heaven after he had come out of this abyss, which contains everything alive. More, there in the ultimate lostness whence all viciousness springs and where all streams of tears have their origin and where the last source of all hatred and self-seeking abides — that is where he has won victory. He won not by shoving the world from himself and heaving it away, but by the fact that, losing himself, he forced his way into the innermost center whence its entire destiny springs forth, seized this center, and accepted it for eternity." *The Great Church Year*, edited by Albert Raffert (New York: Crossroad, 1993), p. 194.

reflected in God's gifts to Teresa and as she perceived them in the world around her.

Today a newly emerging postmodern mysticism moves us to even greater awe before the grandeur of God as we penetrate the secrets of outer space. Planet earth is no longer the center of the universe but minuscule in relation to it. Ecological Theologians like Sally McFague expand our understanding of the grandeur and mystery of God's activity within the world. She envisions the world as God's body.

> As the body of the world, God is forever nailed to the cross, for as the body suffers, so God suffers. Wherever in the universe there is new life, ecstasy, tranquility, and fulfillment, God experiences these pleasures and rejoices with each creature in its joy.[28]

The metaphor of the universe as the body of God, not surprisingly, finds an echo in Teresa. Mystical insight has often been ahead of scientific discovery.[29] In the sixth dwelling places Teresa recounts a vision that makes for a remarkable shift in imagery. Until now the soul is the castle, with God in the center room, the wine cellar of the soul where the soul is inebriated in the embrace of divine union. But something remarkable is now held before us:

> In this vision is revealed how all things are seen *in God* and how God has them all *in Himself.* The evil of of-

---

[28] See *Liberating Life: Contemporary Approaches to Ecological Theology* edited by Charles Birch et al (Maryknoll, NY: Orbis Books, 1990), "Imaging a Theology of Nature: The World as God's Body" by Sally McFague, pp. 201-227.

[29] In 1980 I was an invited guest at an International Symposium entitled "The Monk as Universal Archetype" with Raimundo Panikkar as the main speaker. A brain scientist in my small group made the unforgettable, paradoxical statement: "The mystics were the world's greatest plagiarizers. They said things about the universe sometimes four hundred years before such realities were discovered by scientists."

fending God is seen more clearly, because while *being in God Himself* (I mean *being within Him*) we commit great evils (VI.10.2). [emphasis mine]

Notices how she reiterates: "I mean being within Him" as if to be sure that we get the point. Teresa then continues:

Let's suppose that God is like an immense and beautiful dwelling or palace and that this palace, as I say, is God Himself. Could the sinner, perhaps so as to engage in his evil deeds, leave this palace? No, certainly not; rather within the palace itself, that is within God Himself, the abominations, indecent actions and evil deeds committed by us sinners take place (VI.10.3).

Notice the repetition: "within God Himself." God is now the divine castle. Within God everything for good or for evil runs its course. God is like a global atmosphere, or a global womb in which all that is life-giving and life-destroying occurs. Everything in our world takes place in God. Everything that happens to us, including our distractions, takes place in God. Out of such imagery, I devised what I call my distraction compost heap to take care of the normal flow of distractions, as well as for recurring distracting thoughts that I know refer to something that ultimately needs my attention, but not at the present moment, especially if they come right at the consecration of Mass! I simply acknowledge them without judgment, and then throw them onto my distraction compost heap. I do so, believing that the energy of God, which permeates the universe, will transform what is bothersome to me, into something life-giving for others. If they represent something God wants me to deal with, the distracting thoughts will return, and I will give them proper attention at a more appropriate time. Knowledge and awe before the grandeurs of God help to focus the mind and allure the soul into prayer.

The second sign that Teresa gives here to validate our prayer-experience is growth in self-knowledge and humility (VI.5.10). The soul sees itself in God's light, sinful and lowly "in comparison with the Creator of so many grandeurs" as she puts it. To see oneself before the grandeur of God is first of all to get life into perspective. Difficult things may happen, but they are not the end of the world as the imagination might suggest. God invites us to see all things through the eyes of God, through the lens of ultimate truth, which shines in the heart. In God's light we see ourselves as we can see all the impurities in a glass of water when the sun shines through it. This experience is different from self-depreciation or neurotic guilt. As Teresa says: it leaves virtue, peace, calm and improvement. This dwelling place is the room of truth. We see ourselves in our fragile, finite, sometimes sinful being that exists *within* the being of God who is infinite, compassionate love. The most profound understanding of the first sign: Knowledge of the grandeur of God, is a realization that God's grandeur is precisely that God loves us even in our sinfulness. What is grand about God is that our sometimes sinful, often distracted hearts are not a problem for God.

Teresa's third point for discernment: "Little esteem for earthy things" has a new meaning in our ecological age. Aware that the destruction of earth's natural resources poses increasing dangers to all of us who inhabit our planet, we bring a hermeneutic of suspicion to Teresa's words. Her injunction to have little esteem for earthly things becomes in our ecological age: seeing all things, including nature, from a divine perspective. All things live and move and have their being in God. A sign today of the authenticity of our spiritual experience is a growing esteem, rather than disesteem, for the earth. In God all things are sacred.

To use earthly things for the service of so great a God means for us that we respect the good things of creation as a mode of God's presence and we do not abuse them for our own selfish interests. Over-consumption, mindless waste, thoughtless litter and other forms of earth's desecration call for conversion to a new consciousness of the inter-relatedness between spirit and matter. Dare we suggest that Divine Incarnation extends itself to the full flowering of God's intimate, creating, sustaining, and energizing presence within creation? If the universe might indeed metaphorically be envisioned as the body of God, belief in Christ, along with the sacredness of matter, become integral to each other and to an authentic spiritual life today. We can no longer relate to God in a manner that dissociates us from human and earthly concerns. In the Epilogue to the *Interior Castle*, Teresa draws on nature's bounty to embellish the castle imagery. She writes:

> Although no more than seven dwelling places were discussed, in each of these there are many others... with lovely gardens and fountains and labyrinths, such delightful things that you would want to be dissolved in praises of the great God who created the soul in God's own image and likeness (Epilogue 3).

Any form of ecological abuse is a sin against the body of God, which is the universe, which is Christ, and which is the collective human family. Touches of union in this dwelling place awaken a profound awareness that everything is sacred because everything that is, has been taken up into God, in whom we live and move and have our being, through the death/resurrection of Christ.

As Teresa repeatedly advises us, these sixth dwelling places are about both trials and favors, about dying and rising. These prepare the soul for spiritual espousal with Christ.

Nothing can separate us from God, provided we stay open to God's invitation to a deeper faith through whatever may seem to distract us from God. Even distractions that feel diabolic by their very persistence, by the inner conflict they generate, and by their ability to seemingly divert us from surrender of our life to God, God uses these in the ongoing process of divine transformation.[30] We need continually to return to the meaning of the soul's experiences in these sixth dwelling places. God fashions our person for union with GodSelf. In mystical language this is known as spiritual marriage. Spiritual espousal, as in marriage between persons, is preparatory to this. A deep intimacy already exists between the soul and God. This explains the pain the person feels at seeing oneself so unworthy of this reality and yet so filled with ardent longing. On the one hand are experiences of divine favors; sudden awakenings like a thunderbolt (VI.2.2), wounds of love "as if from the fire enkindled in the brazier that is my God, a spark leapt forth and so struck the soul that flaming fire was felt by it" (VI.2.4),[31] experiences of spiritual fragrance that spreads through all the senses (VI.2.8), locutions (VI.3.1-18), raptures and ecstasies (VI.4.1-17). These are not things of the past. They usually are experienced in less dramatic ways, but if we listen carefully, we might hear a person in spiritual direction say something like this — to give but one example: "I don't know if you could call this a vision, I didn't really see anything, and yet, somehow I did see the heart of God seeming to embrace all peoples everywhere, and I understood deep within, that if I desired to be united with God, I would have to allow God to expand my own heart, to enlarge its ca-

---

[30] "Surrender is not about giving up; it is about moving on," Joan D. Chittester, *Scarred by Struggle, Transformed by Hope* (Grand Rapids, MI: William B. Eerdmans Publishing Company, 2003), p. 59.

[31] See *The Book of Her Life*, 29:10, 13.

pacity, so as to be more all embracing of persons, whether I liked them or not."

Summary

Teresa tells us that these sixth dwelling places are rooms of paradox. Trials and favors accompany one another as the distracting disorders of our perception are purified and re-versioned, so that we can see all things in God. The sixth dwelling places are characterized on the one hand by ardent desires for God, the fruit of God's self-communication, and on the other by experiences of temptation and darkness. It is the place of the dark night. In these dwelling places, Teresa struggles with inner and outer forces that leave her feeling rejected by God, unable to pray, and seeming to suffer the torments of hell.[32] We all forge our own chains, and then unconsciously, begin to worship that which enslaves us. No wonder the devil looms large in the sixth dwelling places. But God also looms even larger as God, with ever greater intensity, draws the heart toward spousal union. The Book of Revelation ends with the final word of God's self-revelation; with the ultimate name for God: *"Behold I make all things new"* (Rv 21:5). The *"I make all things new"* is both a name for God, and God's abiding offer to us. The trials of the sixth dwelling places have to do with the pain of potential. The trials that were integral to Teresa's visions and locutions were God's way of opening Teresa to the vastness of her potential for union with God. God grants the same favor to us. As we have seen, the diamond castle that we are, here undergoes the polishing of God's intimate presence. Everything in one's life that attempts to ex-

---

[32] For her vision of herself in hell see *The Book of Her Life*, 38:1.

ist outside of the divine ambiance becomes the stuff of love's purifying fire. Spiritual betrothal with God in Christ, begins at the first tentative "yes" of conversion from sin, to the rapturous touches of union in these sixth dwelling places. At issue here is our inattentive spirit, our lack of mindfulness. God graciously exposes before the eyes of the soul how deeply rooted attitudes and prejudices chisel away at inclusive, compassionate love, the ultimate fruit of union with God.

Teresa's gift to us today is to help us bear the burden of our incompleteness, and to find in prayer a sacred container that keeps distractions, anxiety and fear from consuming us. Our completion is in God. God is present to both our fullness and our emptiness. God draws us *inward* into the center room — the wine cellar of the deepest self — God also draws us *outward* to embrace all things in God. Everything exists *in God*. The whole of creation, along with persons of every race, color and religious belief, have a home in God.

CHAPTER SEVEN

THE SEVENTH DWELLING PLACES

In these seventh dwelling places, Teresa exposes the deep secrets that lie within the soul (VII.1.1). She is in awe at the task
before her as she begins to write. What she daringly writes about
is nothing less than the marriage of the soul with God as Christ
takes it spiritually, as His spouse: "He brings it into His dwelling
place which is this seventh... where he joins it to Himself"
(VII.1.5). This, however, is a different union from spiritual espousal. It takes place, not in absorption of the faculties, but in
mystical awareness of God's Trinitarian presence, with whom
the soul is united. In spiritual marriage, the Triune God of self-
giving love releases a freedom for service that issues precisely
from the union of the soul with God. Because its motivating
energy is God's own self-giving love, "it seemed to her, despite
the trials she underwent and the business affairs she had to attend to, that the essential part of her soul never moved from that
room" (VII.1.10). This is a different experience from that of spiritual betrothal where "the two can be separated and each remains
by itself." In spiritual marriage, "the soul always remains with
its God in that center" (VII.2.4). Like rain falling into a river,
the two can no longer be separated. Repeatedly does Teresa tell
us that the soul does not move from that center nor is its peace

lost. "Through some secret aspirations the soul understands clearly that it is God who gives life to our soul" (VII.2.6).

Although Teresa tell us that there are none of those movements that usually take place in the faculties and the imagination and do harm to the soul, nor do these stirrings take away its peace, nevertheless, "it should not be thought that the faculties, sense and passions are always in this peace; the soul is, yes. But in those other dwelling places, times of war, trial and fatigue are never lacking; however, they are such that they do not take the soul from its place and its peace; that is, as a rule" (VII.2.10).

The seventh dwelling places are our own personal experience of truly being at home in God. We know without a doubt that we are in God and that God indwells us. We *know* — in the full meaning of that word — that our life plays itself out, moment by moment, held within the embrace of divine love. All of life is perceived, lived and evaluated from these center rooms of rest, which are the seventh dwelling places. One's entire person is now inner directed and sensitively attuned to God's voice, and to the many ways in which God speaks. Everything that we value, which we cherish, our hopes and desires, are seen within the focus and scrutiny of a single-minded and all consuming love for God. An inner light indicates the direction that will keep us on the path of total self-gift.

These are the rooms of peace. Living from these center rooms issues in freedom from the entanglements of life. When we live from our center, the light from within penetrates outward. To live from one's center is to be inner directed. "All things," says Teresa, "must come to the soul from its roots, from where it is planted" (VII.2.9). The tree is planted in the living waters of God and it gives forth abundant fruit. We become one with the heavenly water.

In all of us exists the desire to be peaceful, harmonious, whole and well integrated, and to have a sense of our place in the universe. We would like to be free of our attachments, our addictions and from all that distracts us from being fully present to the moment; in a word, to live in peace. These are worthwhile strivings and anything that helps us toward moral, emotional, psychological and spiritual well-being, is worthwhile. But emotional equilibrium or even the fragile peace we can achieve by our own efforts is not to be identified or confused with living from one's center in the Teresian sense. Teresa describes a transformation that God alone can effect. The peace Teresa describes is the fruit of "our spirit joined in the heavenly union with the uncreated Spirit." In the surrender of human effort, writes Teresa, "everything corporeal in the soul was taken away and it was left in pure spirit" (VII.2.7). The peace that results is possible in the midst of many disturbances in the faculties because its source is outside of their grasp or functioning. "It should not be thought that the faculties, sense and passions are always in this peace; the soul is, yes. But in those other dwelling places, times of war, trial and fatigue are never lacking; however, they are such that they do not take the soul from its peace; that is, as a rule" (VII.2.10). Teresa insists that the peace, the gift of the center dwelling places, is consonant with trials and imperfections. The well-known spiritual writer Henri Nouwen from his own experience assisting the community at L'Arche writes:

> Spiritual rebirth does not necessarily include peace of mind — [peace in the faculties] — it does not necessarily include inner calm, emotional harmony, easy relationships with others and a well-balanced personality. All of these human possibilities may very well characterize a person reborn from above, but none of them makes a truly spiritual person. There are many holy people who are restless, anxious, hard to get along with, and quite unpredictable in their behav-

ior. Often their personalities seem to be at odds with their spiritual call, and often they suffer immensely because they are unable to let their call to live in the Spirit make them psychologically attractive people. Sometimes they seem distant or aloof, uninterested in what we consider real spiritual issues, impatient with our questions and quite asocial. We can see this in the apostles, as well as in many of the men and women whom the church calls saints.[1]

Deep inner holiness, profound surrender, and solid faith can be the ground of a misshapen ill-formed tree. For some persons, the depth of pain that they bear might be too great for them to bring to consciousness, so it gets acted out in difficult or inappropriate behaviors. In such situations, our part is to remain separate and not get entangled in what is not our problem. We challenge or help when this is our responsibility, or when it is the loving thing to do, and we pray for the gift of compassion and humility, since we all bear one another's burdens. We can be very unaware of what others suffer from us. Psychological well-being does not always keep pace with God's activity in the center room. Human limitations do not hinder God's persistent self-communication, although our limitations may confuse and confound our ability to respond according to the heart's deepest desire.

As Teresa reflects on her experience of these seventh dwelling places, she realizes how intensely personal is God's communication with each one of us. Prayer is our human attempt to hear, and in some ways, to see God, and to respond to God with all the love and freedom available to us. God speaks to us even

---

[1] Henri Nouwen, "Reborn from Above" in *Spiritual Life* (Washington, DC: ICS Publications), Spring, 1992.

as God spoke to Teresa, and at times, through the eyes of faith, we do get glimpses of God. We see the face of the suffering Christ in the poor as they reach out for our help; in the pain of people who suffer the ravages of war, as well as in the eyes of persons we hold dear. Our part is to trust God's relentless desire to communicate with us, and to be open to the diversity of God's self-manifestation.

In these seventh dwelling places we become slaves of the crucified. There is no way of being human that does not involve suffering. Mutuality with Christ, the companion of our journey through the dwelling places, brings us to a place of self-giving, so Martha and Mary here join together in mutual service. To respond fully to God means that like Christ, we become a slave of God marked with His brand, which is the cross. Slaves had a particular mark branded into their skin to designate their owner. As children, we were taught that at our Baptism, an indelible mark was left in the soul. We were "Christ-ed" with the pouring of the water and the anointing of oil with the sign of the cross. The cross designates God's ownership of Teresa. "Strive to be the least and slave of all, looking at how or where you can please and serve them" (VII.4.8). Such an attitude is different from being a compulsive "pleaser" or a "push over" needing the approval of others as our source of identity or security. Instead, it means we take the gospel seriously in our following of Jesus.

The inner urgency of the indwelling Trinity whose love cannot be contained, but needs to express itself in mutual exchange of giving, makes it possible for us to go the extra mile in self-giving love. This is very different from compulsive or frenetic doing that leads to burnout. Here again, I suggest that the nature of our distractions will help us to know the difference. If the mind is always racing, and peace in the heart is lacking, we might at least consider whether the energy of our actions is more ego compulsion than Christ motivated. The body may suffer as we travel the extra mile; Teresa admits of many disturbances in the outer rooms of the castle, but in the center the soul is at peace. This peace, the fruit of habitual union with God in the wine cellar of the deepest self, is not affected by turbulence on the seas of life.

Christ's self-giving love reflects itself in Teresa. Her relationship with Christ is one of mutual self-giving. Christ has Teresa understand that "now is the time for her to consider as her own what belongs to Him and that He would take care of what is hers" (VII.2.1; also VII.4.15). Pope John XXIII here comes to mind. At a time of great turmoil in the Church, he stayed peaceful. At night he would say: "It's your Church God, I'm going to sleep." As the father of the prodigal son says to the older brother, Christ says to each one of us, *All that I have is yours.*" Teresa assures us: "His majesty will join our feeble efforts with that which He offered on the cross to the Father for us. Thus even though our works are small, they will have the value our love for Him would have merited, had they been great" (VII.4.15). Teresa learns true discipleship by keeping her eyes fixed on the humanity of Christ. The dryness of our hearts, dreariness before everyday concerns, temptations to hopelessness before the enormity of international violence and injustice, none of these can effectively screen out Christ's creating and re-creating Spirit. Whatever life holds for us is what Christ has already taken hold of and can therefore use for our transformation. This precisely is what the incarnation of God into human life is about. Christ has taken into Himself all that is human so that all that is human is now also of God.

We get a glimpse of what life looked like for Teresa after the grace of spiritual marriage, by turning to *The Book of Her Foundations.* Teresa assures us that in these seventh dwelling places: "There are no interior trials or feelings of dryness, but the soul lives with a remembrance and tender love of our Lord....

When it becomes distracted the Lord himself awakens it in the manner mentioned" (see VI. all of chapter 2; also VII.3.8). Again she writes: "There are almost never any experiences of dryness or interior disturbance of the kind that were present at times in all the other dwelling places, but the soul is almost always in quiet" (VII.3.10). However, as we read accounts of her foundations, the picture changes. One of her most difficult foundations was that of Seville in the southern part of Spain, in the province of Andalusia. Here she encountered great difficulties. Scorching heat, high fever, miserable accommodations, and dangerous river crossings, were the least of her trials. Difficulties with the Archbishop, difficulties in finding a house suited to their needs, etc., have Teresa comment that none of her foundations cost her as much as this one (BF 26.2). She suffered fears, even "great fear" (BF 28.14), and at times temptations to both "fear and doubt" (BF 28.19). She mentions feeling distressed, and having anxiety over seemingly overwhelming problems. When asked to make the foundation in Burgos, she comments, "I couldn't bear the thought of going to a place as cold as Burgos with so many illnesses aggravated by the cold" (BF 31.11). From 1572 when Teresa received the grace of spiritual marriage, until her death in 1582, she visited 57 cities of Castile and Andalusia in the process of making foundations, or visiting ones that needed help. One can only imagine the inconveniences of traveling rough terrain on a donkey or in a mule drawn cart through heat and cold with all of these conditions exacerbated by almost continual illness.

All of this reminds us that spiritual marriage does not take the person into ethereal realms of unreality.

> You may think that as a result the soul will be outside itself and so absorbed that it will be unable to be occupied with anything else. On the contrary, the soul

is much more occupied than before with everything pertaining to the service of God; and once its duties are over it remains with enjoyable company (VII.1.8).

Life continues — although in a sense, nothing is the same since the soul remains at peace in the center rooms of the castle although not a peace without disturbance in the outer rooms of the castle. For as Teresa tells us:

> You must not think, sisters, that the effects I mentioned (VII.3.2-10) are always present in these souls. Hence, where I remember, I say "ordinarily." For sometimes our Lord leaves these individuals in their natural state, and then it seems all the poisonous creatures from the outskirts and other dwelling places of this castle band together to take revenge for the time they were unable to have these souls under their control (VII.4.1).

We might conclude from this that the person encounters distractions characteristic of the other dwelling places, but that these "last only a short time … and the soul's gain through the good company it is in becomes manifest. For the Lord gives the soul great stability and good resolutions not to deviate from His service in anything" (VII.4.2). Distractions and temptations are always with us. But here there is a difference. God's Trinitarian presence in the center rooms so grounds the soul and holds it in loving communion, that all of life's sufferings and trials now become occasions for closer identification with the Crucified. Her eyes unrelentingly fixed on the Crucified, Teresa sees with certitude the meaning of her life at this time in her spiritual journey:

It means becoming the slaves of God. Marked with his brand, which is that of the cross, spiritual persons because now they have given Him their liberty, can be sold by Him as slaves of everyone as he was (VII.4.8).

We might ask: are distractions ever put to rest? It seems not. Teresa herself addresses the question:

I have already told you that the calm these souls have interiorly is for the sake of their having much less calm exteriorly and much less desire to have exterior calm (VII.4.10).

Teresa says that the passions are here conquered, which means inordinate desires are no longer in control. However, inevitable psychic limitations, unexamined attitudes formed by a culture and family life, instinctive emotions, etc., as well as difficult life situations, continue to distract the soul. Again, the difference is that "the soul now wages more war from the center than it did when it was outside suffering with them, for then it did not understand the tremendous gain trials bring.... The soul is now fortified with the strength it has from drinking wine in this wine cellar where its Spouse has brought it.... From these center rooms, strength flows back to the weak body as the soul becomes increasingly stronger" (VII.4.10-11). Here, dealing with distractions is not one's concern, but rather, how better to serve. Repeatedly does Teresa affirm that the purpose of these seventh dwelling places is good works:

This is the reason for the prayer, my daughters, the purpose of this spiritual marriage: the birth of good works, good works (VII.4.6).

This is what I want you to strive for, my sisters, and let us desire and be occupied in prayer not for the sake of our enjoyment but so as to have this strength to serve (VII.4.12).

When the nuns object that they are unable to bring souls to God, Teresa counters with solid advice "…you need not be desiring to benefit the whole world but must concentrate on those who are in your company, and thus your deed will be greater since you are more obliged toward them" (VII.4.14). In other words, opportunities for service can be found right within the inevitable boundaries that limit each person's life. The distractions that such service occasions become opportunities for deeper humility and a deeper surrender of oneself to God in trust and confidence. We simply move on, knowing that "the Lord doesn't look so much at the greatness of our works as at the love with which they are done" (VII.4.15).

OVERVIEW AND SUMMARY

Teresa's seven dwelling places attempt to name the human experience in its journey of discovering all things in God. Each of the dwelling places reveals both the wonders of God's self-communicating love and the chaotic tendencies of the self toward dissipation and distraction. The true self is realized not by grit of achievement, but as gift. God is the one who draws the soul into the wine cellar of the heart where the union of God and the human is celebrated. The self blossoms not as a hectic enterprise, but in communion with God. God is self-giving communion. We become ourselves in the gift of self to God that in turn enables genuine self-giving communion with others. Teresa's dwelling places are like a mystical map that both charts our journey and alerts us when we are off course.

The first dwelling places are the site of superficial living. We live outside of the true self without reference to God.

The second dwelling places hold the invitation to the "more" of life: to moral conversion that allows the indwelling God to become intimate to the whole of one's life journey.

In the third dwelling places, things look good on the outside; we do the Christian thing — we pray, go to church, etc. But inside exists a roomful of smugness and self-satisfaction where in its extreme, self-righteous rigid conservatives and self-righteous rigid liberals find a breeding place. Both positions rigidly adhered to, wait the tempering of contemplative surrender to both the mysterious complexities of life and to God as ultimate mystery. In the third dwelling places, God invites us to intellectual conversion so that the mind can begin to see reality through the compassionate eyes of God. The truth that is humility is a standing invitation "to join the human race," and to acknowledge the limitations both of our supposed holiness, and of how we view both Church and world. What we see is but partial reality.

In the fourth dwelling places God initiates a specific self-communication known as contemplation. The only adequate response on our part is toward letting go of control in prayer and in the everydayness of life. In prayer, we learn surrender within the dryness of faith, and through the consolation of spiritual delight.

The fifth dwelling places are characterized by brief experiences of union with God from which issues a spiritual rebirth. Filled with God's creative energy, the silkworm spins the cocoon and dies in the hope of a resurrected life, and a rebirth in the beauty of God.

The sixth dwelling places are the rooms of the dark night as God's desire to communicate with us meets human resistance. Through a purified sensitivity to God's visitations, we come better to prize the mystery that is ourselves. The eyes and ears of the soul are opened to see and to hear God in the everydayness of life as Teresa did through her visions and locutions. As we increasingly see all things *in God*, attachments to things of this world tend to fall away because they no longer have the same meaning for us. We can use them and enjoy them without attachment. We have come to inner freedom and to the liberty of the children of God.

In the seventh dwelling places we finally find our true home in Christ. The heart of Christ is now our abiding place of rest. In Christ is found a peace that nothing disturbs. In Christ is also discovered a powerful source of energy for service as Christ's concerns become ours. These are the rooms of harmony and integration. All of life's sufferings, pains of the body, the hurts of injustice and the wounds of envy and thoughtlessness, all serve to deepen humility and gospel living. They also become transparencies of God. Going the extra mile, turning the other cheek and forgiving seventy times seven have new meaning within the Trinitarian event of expressive love. None of life's disturbing injustices and inequities shakes one's peace when we are united with God in our deepest center. From this center we gain clarity for appropriate action.

From Teresa's dwelling places we learn that what constitutes us as persons and that gives us identity, is not the body/psyche existence that is uniquely ours, but our relationship with God. God loves us with a passionate singularity that calls us — we who cannot exist without God — into existence.[1] God, as self-communicating Trinitarian love, establishes us in our personal otherness as image of God. God's inviting love makes possible our own passionate response to the call of God who draws us into the divine Trinitarian person/relational existence. To truly image God is to be for others as God is for us. In Christ, we live our human nature into authentic personhood by being the beloved of God and by speaking God's eternal word in the very mundane details of everyday human life. Insofar as we turn away from, or resist God's ever present, person-constituting call, do

---

[1] Rm 4:17. "As Scripture says: 'I have made you the ancestor of many nations.' Abraham is our father in the eyes of God in whom he put his faith, and who brings the dead to life and calls into being what did not exist."

we fall prey to the self-preserving preoccupations that are at the heart of much that distracts us in prayer.

What distracts us in prayer, or in daily living, usually is subtle, human resistance to God's divinizing process. But we can also consider distractions from another perspective. As image of God, our relational existence encompasses the whole of us. Everything within and without exists in relation to something else. As Paul puts it, no part of the body can say: "I have no need of you." Our participation in the dynamic, relational energies of Trinitarian *loving in the other* finds reflection in a lame and disjointed way, through the mind's persistent flow toward what is other than itself. Rather than being disturbed by our distractions, by the mind's persistent flow of thought, we can look on our distractions with awe — as reflective of a deeper mystery. While they keep us rooted in the reality of our finite existence with the broken fragments of our scattered psyche, in this there is cause for rejoicing. Everything that constitutes our humanity has been taken up, through the humanity of Christ, into the communion of life that is God.

The divine Trinitarian communion may shroud us in dark night but this is a night "more lovely than the dawn." On the one hand, darkness is a sign of all that separates us from God; but on the other, on the level of mysticism, darkness is the face of God's self-disclosure, as when God appeared to the Israelites in the dark cloud at Sinai. Darkness happens because the mind is confronted with something beyond the conceivable: God's self-communicating love. God draws the mind into realms of possibilities it could never have imagined. Who would dare to think that we humans could aspire to an intimate union with God! God, who on the one hand is the source of our deepest desires, is, on the other, sheer darkness to the intellect. No wonder that the intellect wanders off for more substantial substance to ruminate.

The same reality actually holds true for the root of our identity, which is hidden from us, because it is hidden in God, in the wine cellar where God's love holds us in existence. Denys Turner in his book *The Darkness of God* says it well:

> Our deepest center, the most intimate source from which our actions flow, our freedom to love, is in us but not of us, is not "ours" to possess, but ours only to be possessed by. And so faith at once "de-centers" us for it disintegrates the experiential structures of selfhood on which, in experience, we center ourselves, and at the same time draws us into the divine love where we are "re-centered" upon a ground beyond any possibility of experience.[2]

The lure of God is what actualizes our transcendent potential. The highest or deepest level of divine presence to the soul is always in luminous darkness, an unknowing that yet stirs an insatiable desire. All that is other than God, God transforms into God-by-participation. This process confounds the intellect. The silence of mystical speech is the effect of God's superabundant self-communication. The intellect and imagination go off after their own satisfaction in conceivable thoughts and images before the inconceivability of God.

All of created reality is an access to God and our spirit is meant to know and enjoy created things. That they ensnare us, that we become attached to them, so that they become occasions of sin, or excessive preoccupation through distracting thoughts, is the human perversion of God's intent. In traditional language, this reality is known as original sin.

---

[2] Denys Truner, *The Darkness of God: Negativity in Christian Mysticism* (Cambridge, MA: Cambridge University Press, 1995), p. 251.

, When we are distracted by our distractions, Teresa's dwelling places offer us a guide to deeper self-knowledge precisely through our distractions. Through them we can become in touch with deeply entrenched manners of being, thinking and relating. Teresa's insights to the dwelling places of the soul, alert us to the meaning of our distractions. God invites us to inner freedom and to a deeper surrender of our lives to God. Instead of being a curse, distractions become a blessing — a visitation from God. God speaks through our persistent distracting thoughts. Through them, God invites us to look more closely at the things we value. What changes are not the objects we see through our eyes, but our eyes themselves are given, as it were, divine lenses, so that we see all things through the eyes of God. Our heart, united with the heart of God, makes possible a new, divine way of seeing as a vision of the heart. Our distractions, quietly reflected upon, can connect us more deeply with Christ and the Trinitarian God of Christian revelation. They can open us to a deeper understanding of how God's self-communication in the soul confounds human consciousness, and challenges the intellect to a deepened faith. Having completed our journey through the seven dwelling places, and having looked at distractions and their meaning through the prism of the seven dwelling places of Teresa's *Interior Castle*, hopefully, we can now listen with fresh insight to the voices of our distractions, and perhaps even welcome them as integral to God's transforming process.

BIBLIOGRAPHY

Blommestijn, Hem, Huts Jos, Waaijman, Kees. *The Footprints of Love: John of the Cross as Guide in the Wilderness*, translated by John Vriend (Louvain, Belgium: Peeters, 2000).

Burrows, Ruth. *Interior Castle Explored* (London & Dublin: Sheed & Ward/Veritas Publications, 1981).

Chapman, John. *Spiritual Letters* (London, 1935).

Chittester, Joan D. *Scarred by Struggle, Transformed by Hope* (Grand Rapids, MI: William B. Eerdmans Publishing Co., 2003).

Coakley, Sarah. *Powers and Submissions: Spirituality, Philosophy and Gender* (Maiden, MA: Blackwell Publishers, 2002).

Damasio, Antonio. *The Feeling of What Happens: Body and Emotions in the Making of Consciousness* (San Diego, New York, London: A Harvest Book, Harcourt, Inc., 1999).

Egan, Keith J., editor. *Carmelite Prayer: A Tradition for the 21st Century* (New York/Mahwah, NJ: Paulist Press, 2003).

Eliade, Mircea. *A History of Religious Ideas*, translated by Willard R. Trask. (Chicago: University of Chicago Press, 1982).

Gendlin, Eugene, Ph.D. *Focusing* (New York: Bantam Books, 1981).

Hunt, Anne. *New Theology Studies 5: The Trinity and the Paschal Mystery: A development in Recent Catholic Theology* (Collegeville, MN: The Liturgical Press, 1997).

John of the Cross, St. *The Collected Works of St. John of the Cross*, trans. Kieran Kavanaugh, OCD, and Otilio Rodriguez, OCD (Washington, DC: ICS Publications, 1991).

Keating, Thomas. *Intimacy with God: Transformation through Contemplation* (New York: Crossroad, 1994).

Levinas, Emmanuel. *Otherwise than Being or Beyond Essence*, trans. by Alphonso Lingis (Dordrecht: Kluwer Academic Publishers, 1991).

Lonergan, Bernard. *Method in Theology* (New York: Seabury Press, 1972).

Luke, Helen. *Dark Wood, White Rose* (Pecos, NM: Dove Publications, 1975).

Matthew, Iain. *The Impact of God* (London: Hodder & Stoughton, 1995).

May, Gerald. *Will and Spirit: A Contemplative Psychology* (San Francisco: Harper and Row, 1982).

McFague, Sally. *Liberating Life: Contemporary Approaches to Ecological Theology*, edited by Charles Birch, et al (Maryknoll, NY: Orbis Books, 1990).

_____. *The Body of God: An Ecological Theology* (Minneapolis, MN: Fortress Press, 1993).

_____. *Life Abundant: Rethinking Theology and Economy for A Planet in Peril* (Minneapolis, MN: Fortress Press, 2001).

McIntosh, Mark. *Mystical Theology: The Integrity of Spirituality and Theology* (Maiden, MA: Blackwell Publishers, 1998).

Moore, Sebastian. *The Fire and the Rose Are One* (New York: Seabury Press, 1980).

Nouwen, Henri. "Reborn from Above," in *Spiritual Life* (Washington, DC: ICS Publications, Spring issue, 1992).

Rahner, Karl. "Experience of Self and Experience of God" in *Theological Investigations*, Vol. 13 (New York: Crossroad, 1983).

_____. *The Great Church Year*, edited by Albert Raffelt, (New York: Crossroad, 1993).

_____. *The Practice of Faith: Handbook of Contemporary Spirituality* (New York: Crossroad, 1986).

Rizzuto, M.D., Ana-Maria. *The Birth of the Living God: A Psychoanalytic Study* (Chicago: University of Chicago Press, 1981).

Seelaus, Vilma, OCD. "Crisis and Transformation: Turning Over the Compost Heap," in *The Way* (London: Heythrop College, January, 2004).

_____. "The Self: Mirror of God," in *The Way* (London: Heythrop College, July, 1992).

_____. "The Self in Postmodern Thought: A Carmelite Response," in *Review for Religious* (St. Louis, MO: September-October 1999).

_____. "Teresa Revisions Humility: A Matter of Justice," in *The Land of Carmel: Essays in Honor of Joachim Smet, O.Carm.* edited by Paul Chandler, O.Carm. & Keith Egan (Rome: Institutum Carmelitanum, Via Sforza Pallavicini, 10, 1991).

Swimme, Brian. *The Universe is a Green Dragon: A Cosmic Creation Story* (Santa Fe, NM: Bear & Co., 1984).

Talbot, Michael. *The Holographic Universe* (New York: Harper Perennial, 1992).

Teresa of Avila, St. *The Collected Works of St. Teresa of Avila* (3 volumes), trans. Kieran Kavanaugh, OCD, and Otilio Rodriguez, OCD (Washington, DC: ICS Publications, 1976, 1980, 1985).

Thérèse of Lisieux, St. *Story of a Soul: The Autobiography of St. Thérèse of Lisieux*, 3rd ed.; trans. John Clarke, OCD (Washington, DC: ICS Publications, 1996).

Turner, Denys. *The Darkness of God: Negativity in Christian Mysticism* (Cambridge, MA: Cambridge University Press, 1995).

Van Beeck, Frans Jozef, S.J. *Christ Proclaimed: Christology as Rhetoric* (New York: Paulist Press, 1979).

Verge, Charles, Ph.D. "Foundations for a Spiritually Based Psychotherapy," in *Religion and Family*, edited by L. Burton (Hayworth Press, 1992).

Wink, Walter. *Unmasking the Powers: The Invisible Forces That Determine Human Existence* (Philadelphia: Fortress Press, 1986).

ST PAULS

This book was produced by ST PAULS/Alba House, the Society of St. Paul, an international religious congregation of priests and brothers dedicated to serving the Church through the communications media.

For information regarding this and associated ministries of the Pauline Family of Congregations, write to the Vocation Director, Society of St. Paul, P.O. Box 189, 9531 Akron-Canfield Road, Canfield, Ohio 44406-0189. Phone (330) 702-0359; or E-mail: spvocationoffice@aol.com or check our internet site, www.albahouse.org